Your Malvern Gui
for GCSE

German
Vocabulary

Val Levick
Glenise Radford
Alasdair McKeane

Titles available
from
Malvern Language Guides:

French	German	Spanish	Italian
Vocabulary Guide	Vocabulary Guide	Vocabulary Guide	Vocabulary Guide
Speaking Test Guide	Speaking Test Guide	Speaking Test Guide	Speaking Test Guide
Essential Verbs	Essential Verbs		
Grammar Guide	Grammar Guide	Grammar Guide	Grammar Guide
French Dictionary	German Dictionary		
Mon Echange Scolaire	Mein Austausch	Mi Intercambio Escolar	
Ma Visite En France			
Key Stage 3 Guide	Key Stage 3 Guide	Key Stage 3 Guide	
CE 13+ French			
Standard Grade French			

(Order form inside the back of this book - photocopy and return)

CONTENTS

Please note the following points:

- * These verbs take **sein** in the perfect and other compound tenses

- (*) These verbs can take **sein** or **haben** in the perfect and other compound tenses

- *sep* These verbs have a *sep*arable prefix

- *insep* These verbs have an *insep*arable prefix

- † These verbs are broadly regular, but have variations in some tenses.
  For further information refer to our publication 'Essential German Verbs'

- *irreg These* verbs are *irreg*ular. In lists where **an irregular verb** occurs more than once only the first one is marked *irreg*

- *s.o* This means someone

- *o.s* This means oneself

- *pl* indicates that the noun is given in its plural form

- *no pl* indicates that the noun does not have a plural form

- *no sing* indicates that the noun does not have a singular form

- *wk* indicates that the noun is a weak noun

- ‡ indicates that the noun is an adjectival noun

- For reasons of space the feminine version of a person or profession is often not given where it is formed by adding -in (nen) to the masculine noun

- *coll* indicates that the word is colloquial or slang

- *inv* indicates that the adjective never changes

- Page references are made at the end of sections to indicate other words which might be useful to the topic

- To avoid repetition, common verbs, adjectives, adverbs, prepositions, conjunctions, question words, numbers, dates and times are in lists on pages 80-87

- Opinions and justifications are on pages 78-79

Produced using Duden Rechtschreibung 21. Ausgabe and associated publications

MY WORLD

1A SELF, FAMILY AND FRIENDS

Die Familie und Freunde
Family and friends

der Bruder (Brüder) ......brother
das Einzelkind (er)........only child
die Eltern *pl* ....parents
die Frau (en) ....wife
die Geschwister *pl* ....brothers and sisters
der Mann (Männer) ......husband
die Mutter (Mütter) ......mother
die Mutti (s).................mummy
die Schwester (n)..........sister
der Sohn (Söhne)..........son
die Tochter (Töchter) ...daughter
der Vater (Väter)..........father
der Vati (s)...................daddy

das Baby (s) ....baby
der Cousin (s) ....male cousin
die Cousine (n) ....female cousin
die Großeltern *pl* ....grandparents
die Großmutter (-mütter)..grandmother
der Großvater (-väter)...grandfather
der Halbbruder (-brüder) ..half brother
die Halbschwester (n)...half sister
die Kusine (n)...............female cousin
die Oma/Omi (s)..........granny
der Onkel (-) ....uncle
der Opa/Opi (s)............grandpa
der Partner (-) ....partner
die Partnerin (nen).......partner
die Stiefmutter (-mütter) .... stepmother
der Stiefvater (-väter) ...stepfather
die Tante (n) ....aunt
die Zwillinge *pl* ....twins

der Enkel (-).................grandson
die Enkelin (nen) ....granddaughter

das Enkelkind (er) .... grandchild
der Neffe (n) *wk* .... nephew
die Nichte (n) .... niece
der Schwager (Schwäger) ......brother-in-law
die Schwägerin (nen) ....sister-in-law
die Schwiegermutter (-mütter)
....mother-in-law
der Schwiegersohn (-söhne)...son-in-law
die Schwiegertochter (-töchter)
....daughter-in-law
der Schwiegervater (-väter)....father-in-law
der Stiefsohn (-söhne) ....stepson
die Stieftochter (-töchter).......stepdaughter
der Vetter (n)................ male cousin

die Dame (n) .... lady
die Frau (en)................ woman
der Freund (e).............. friend, boyfriend
die Freundin (nen)........ friend, girlfriend
der Bekannte (n) ‡........ friend
der Herr (en) *wk* .... gentleman
der Junge (n) *wk* .... boy
das Kind (er)................ child
die Leute *pl* .... people
das Mädchen (-)........... girl
der Mann (Männer) ...... man
der Nachbar (n) *wk* .... neighbour
die Nachbarin (nen)...... neighbour

der Alleinstehende (n) ‡... single man
die Alleinstehende (n) ‡... single woman
der Ausländer (-) .... foreigner
die Ausländerin (nen)... foreigner
der Brieffreund (e) .... penfriend
die Brieffreundin (nen) penfriend
der Erwachsene (n) ‡.... adult
der Fremde (n) ‡.......... foreigner, stranger
der Geschiedene (n) ‡ ..divorcee

1

der Junggeselle (n) *wk* . bachelor
der Jugendliche (n) ‡ ... teenager, young person
der Verlobte (n) ‡ .... fiancé
die Verlobte (n) ‡ .... fiancée
der Verwandte (n) ‡..... relative

die junge Generation ... the younger generation
der Rentner (-) .... retired person
die Senioren *pl*............ senior citizens
die Witwe (n).............. widow
der Witwer (-)............. widower

die Kindheit .... childhood
die Jugend.................. youth

Wie ist er/sie?   **What is he/she like?**
Adoptif- .... adopted
alt .... aged, elderly, old
älter............................ older, elder
Familien-.................... of the family
geschieden .... divorced
getrennt .... separated
jünger......................... younger
ledig........................... single, unmarried
unverheiratet .... single, unmarried
verheiratet.................. married
verlobt........................ engaged
verwitwet .... widowed

anglikanisch .... anglican
atheistisch .... atheist
christlich .... Christian
evangelisch .... Protestant
hindu.......................... Hindu
jüdisch .... Jewish
katholisch................... Catholic
mohammedanisch .... Muslim
sikhisch...................... Sikh
ohne Konfession .... of no religion

Die Haustiere   **Pets**
der Goldfisch (e)......... goldfish
der Hamster (-)............ hamster

das Haustier (e)............ pet
der Hund (e) .... dog
die Hündin (nen) .... bitch
der junge Hund............ puppy
das Kaninchen (-) .... rabbit
der Kater (-)................. tom-cat
das Kätzchen (-)........... kitten
die Katze (n)................ cat
die Maus (Mäuse) .... mouse
das Meerschweinchen (-).. guinea pig
der Papagei (en)........... parrot
das Pferd (e)................ horse
die Schildkröte (n)........ tortoise
das Tier (e)................... animal
der Vogel (Vögel)......... bird
der Wellensittich (e)..... budgerigar
die Wüstenspringmaus (-mäuse). gerbil

dressieren † .... to train
füttern......................... to feed
ein Tier halten *irreg* ..... to keep an animal
pfeifen *irreg* .... to whistle

Die Identität   **Identity**
  Frau .... Mrs, Ms
  Fräulein .... Miss
  Herr (en) *wk*........... Mr
die Adresse (n) .... address
die Anschrift (en) .... address
der Ausweis (e) .... identity card, ID
der Familienname (n) *wk*.. surname
die Faxnummer (n)....... fax number
  geboren am … .... born on …
das Geburtsdatum .... date of birth
der Geburtsort (e) .... place of birth
das Geschlecht (er) .... sex, gender
die Größe (n) .... height, size
die Hausnummer (n) .... house number
der Nachname (n) *wk*.... surname
der Name (n) *wk* .... name
der Ort (e)................... place
der Pass (Pässe) .... passport

2

der Personalausweis (e) .....identity card
die Postleitzahl (en)......postcode
der Spitzname (n) *wk*....nickname
die Staatsangehörigkeit .....nationality
die Stadt (Städte)..........town
die Straße (n)................street, road
die Telefonnummer (n) .....phone number
die Unterschrift (en) .....signature
der Vorname (n) *wk*......first name
der Wohnort (e) ....place of residence

wohnen ....to live (reside)
buchstabieren † ....to spell

Alter   **Age**
das Alter ....age, old age
das Datum (Daten) ....date
die Geburt (en)............birth
der Geburtstag (e)........birthday
das Jahr (e) ....year
das Leben.....................life
der Monat (e)...............month

männlich................male
weiblich.................female
minderjährig..........minor, under 18
volljährig...............adult, over 18

Phrases

Ich heiße David. Ich bin sechzehn Jahre alt *My name is David. I am 16*
Ich wohne in Worcester *I live in Worcester*
Wie schreibt man das? *How do you spell that?*
Ich habe am neunzehnten Mai Geburtstag *My birthday is May 19th*
Ich bin neunzehnhundertachtundachtzig in York geboren *I was born in York in 1988*
Ich bin Engländer/Ire/Schotte/Waliser *I am English/Irish/Scottish/Welsh (and male)*
Ich bin Engländerin/Irin/Schottin/Waliserin *I am English/Irish/Scottish/Welsh (and female)*
Ich komme aus der BRD/Bundesrepublik *I come from Germany*
Ich habe einen Bruder und zwei Schwestern *I have one brother and two sisters*
Ich bin Einzelkind *I am an only child*
Mein Vater ist Bäcker, meine Mutter ist Lehrerin *My father is a baker, my mother is a teacher*
Meine Eltern sind geschieden *My parents are divorced*
Ich verstehe mich gut mit meinem Bruder *I get on well with my brother*

Das Aussehen   **Appearance**
die Augen *pl* ....eyes
der Bart (Bärte)............beard
die Brille (n) ....pair of glasses
die Glatze (n)...............bald patch
die Haare *pl* ....hair
der Oberlippenbart (-bärte).... moustache
der Pony (s).................fringe

blass............................pale
blond...........................blonde
dick ....fat
dünn ....thin

frisiert..........................curly (frizzy)
glatt ....straight (hair)
hässlich........................ugly
hübsch ....pretty
lockig ....curly (wavy)
mittelgroß....................of average height
rothaarig ....red-haired
schlank ....slim
stark............................strong
untersetzt.....................stocky
weiß............................white

wiegen *irreg*................to weigh

3

Berufe   Professions

NB The feminine version of a profession is not
given where it is formed by adding **-in (nen)**
to the masculine noun.

der Arzt (Ärzte) .... doctor

die Ärztin (nen) .... doctor

der Beamte (n) ‡ .... civil servant, official

der Berater (-) .... counsellor

der Chirurg (en) *wk* ..... surgeon

der Feuerwehrmann (Feuerwehrleute)
.... fireman

der Krankenpfleger (-) . male nurse

die Krankenschwester (n) ..nurse

der Lehrer (-)............... teacher

der Politiker (-) .... politician

der Polizist (en) *wk* ..... policeman

der Schulleiter (-)........ headteacher

der Sozialarbeiter (-).... social worker

der Tierarzt (-ärzte)...... vet (fem like Arzt)

der Zahnarzt (-ärzte) .... dentist (fem like Arzt)

der Architekt (en) *wk* ... architect

der Ausbilder (-) .... instructor

der Autor (en) *wk*........ writer

der Bibliothekar (e)...... librarian

der Büroangestellte ‡ ... office worker

der Chef (s) .... boss

der Designer (-)........... designer

der Dolmetscher (-)...... interpreter

der Forscher (-) .... research worker

die Geschäftsfrau (en).. businesswoman

der Geschäftsmann (-männer)... businessman

der Informatiker (-) ...... computer scientist

der Ingenieur (e) .... engineer

der Journalist (en) *wk*... journalist

die Kauffrau (en) .... businesswoman

der Kaufmann .... businessman

die Kaufleute *pl* .... businessmen

der Meteorologe (n) *wk*.....meteorologist

der Moderator (en)....... TV presenter

der Musiker (-)............. musician

der Naturwissenschaftler (-).. scientist

der Programmierer (-)...programmer

der Rechtsanwalt (-anwälte).. lawyer

die Rechtsanwältin (nen)....... lawyer

der Steuerberater (-) ..... accountant

der Techniker (-).......... technician

der Vertreter (-) .... rep(resentative)

der Apotheker (-)......... chemist (dispensing)

der Bäcker (-) .... baker

der Drogist (en) *wk*...... chemist (non-dispensing)

der Fischhändler (-)...... fishmonger

der Fleischer (-) .... butcher

der Florist (en) *wk* .... florist

der Fotograf (en) *wk* ..... photographer

die Friseuse (n)............. hairdresser

der Frisör (e)................ hairdresser

der Gemüsehändler (-).. greengrocer

der Hotelbesitzer (-) ..... hotelier

der Kassierer (-)........... till operator, cashier

der Ladenbesitzer (-) ....shopkeeper

der Metzger (-) .... butcher

der Obsthändler (-) .... fruitseller

der Verkäufer (-)........... sales assistant

der Wohnungsmakler (-) ...estate agent

der Zeitungshändler (-)...... newsagent

der Bauarbeiter (-) .... construction worker

der Briefträger (-) .... postman

der Elektriker (-).......... electrician

der Fahrer (-) .... driver

die Hausfrau (en)......... housewife

der Hausmann (-männer).. house-husband

der Handwerker (-) .... craftsman, tradesman

der Kellner (-).............. waiter

der Koch (Köche)......... cook

die Köchin (nen) .... cook

der Maurer (-) .... bricklayer

der Mechaniker (-)........ mechanic

die Sekretärin (nen)...... secretary

der Tischler (-)............. carpenter

der Arbeiter (-) .... manual worker
der Bauer (n) *wk* .... farmer
der Bauunternehmer (-) ..... builder
der Bergmann (Bergleute) . miner
der Fischer (-) .... fisherman
der Flugbegleiter (-) ...... flight attendant
der Gärtner (-) .... gardener
der Hausmeister (-) .... caretaker
das Kindermädchen (-) . nanny
der Klempner (-) .... plumber
der Maler (-) .... painter
der Matrose (n) *wk* .... sailor
der Pilot (en) *wk* .... pilot
der Sänger (-) .... singer
der Soldat (en) *wk* .... soldier

Der Arbeitsplatz   The workplace

das Büro (s) .... office
die Fabrik (en) .... factory
die Firma (Firmen) .... firm
das Geschäft (e) .... shop
das Krankenhaus (-häuser) .... hospital
das Labor (s) .... laboratory
der Laden (Läden) .... shop
die Schule (n) .... school

drinnen .... outdoors
draußen .... indoors

Begrüßungen   Exchanging greetings

Guten Morgen! .... Good Morning
Guten Tag! .... Good Afternoon
Guten Abend! .... Good Evening
Hallo! .... Hi
Auf Wiedersehen! .... Goodbye
Tschüs! .... Goodbye
Grüß dich! .... Hello
Grüß Gott! .... Hello
Servus! .... Hi/Goodbye
Bis bald! .... See you soon
Bis später! .... See you later
Bis morgen! .... See you tomorrow

Wie geht's? .... How are you?
Gut, danke .... Very well, thank you
Mittelmäßig .... So-so
Darf ich Eva vorstellen? .. May I introduce Eva?
Angenehm .... Pleased to meet you

Herzlich willkommen! . Welcome!
Herein! .... Come in
Nehmen Sie Platz! .... Sit down
Bitte .... Please
Danke .... Thank you
Entschuldigen Sie! .... Excuse me

kennen lernen .... to meet s.o.

Als Gast   Being a guest

der Brieffreund (e) .... penfriend (m)
die Brieffreundin (nen) penfriend (f)
der Gast (Gäste) .... guest (m)
der Gastgeber (-) .... host
die Gastgeberin (nen) ... hostess

das Geschenk (e) .... present
der Koffer (-) .... suitcase
die Reisetasche (n) .... holdall
die Seife .... soap
das Shampoo .... shampoo
die Wolldecke (n) .... blanket
die Zahnbürste (n) .... toothbrush
die Zahnpasta .... toothpaste

deutsch .... German
englisch .... English
irisch .... Irish
österreichisch .... Austrian
schottisch .... Scottish
schweizerisch .... Swiss
walisisch .... Welsh

älter .... elder, older
freundlich .... welcoming
jünger .... younger
schüchtern .... shy

5

abfahren* *irreg sep* ...... to leave, depart

ankommen* *irreg sep* .. to arrive

ausgehen* *irreg sep* ..... to go out

ausleihen *irreg sep* .... to borrow

begrüßen † .... to greet

brauchen .... to need

danken (+ Dat) .... to thank

empfangen *irreg* .... to receive (guest)

willkommen heißen *irreg* ..to welcome

lächeln .... to smile

leihen *irreg* .... to lend

schenken .... to give (present)

Deutsch sprechen *irreg* ...... to speak German

Englisch sprechen *irreg*...... to speak English

For **opinions** see page 78

Phrases

Vielen Dank für alles *Thank you for everything*

Ich habe wunderschöne Ferien verbracht *I've had a wonderful holiday*

Sie waren/Du warst so freundlich *You have been so kind*

Bedanke dich bei deinen Eltern für mich, bitte *Say thank you to your parents for me, please*

Ich möchte dich gern wieder besuchen *I'd love to come and see you again*

Schreib bald! *Write soon!*

1B   INTERESTS AND HOBBIES

Der Sport   Sport

die Atmosphäre ....atmosphere
die Ferien *pl*.................holidays
die Freizeit...................free time
das Hobby (s)...............hobby
die Sportart (en)...........(type of) sport
die Unterhaltung...........entertainment
das Wochenende (n) .....weekend

der Fan (s)....................fan, supporter
die Mannschaft (en)......team
der Meister (-)..............champion
die Meisterin (nen) ....champion
das Mitglied (er) ....member
der Profi (s)..................professional
der Schiedsrichter (-)....referee
der Spieler (-)...............player
die Spielerin (nen) ....player

der Fußballverein (e) ....football club
der Platz (Plätze) ....pitch, court
der Sportplatz (-plätze)......sports ground
das Sportzentrum (-zentren) .. sports centre
das Stadion (Stadien)....stadium
der Tennisclub (s).........tennis club

das Endspiel (e) ....final
die Liga (Ligen)............league
die Gebühr (en) ....fee
die Meisterschaft (en)...championship
das Spiel (e) ....match, game
das Tor (e)....................goal
das Turnier (e) ....tournament
der Wettbewerb (e).......competition, contest
unentschieden ....drawn

Welchen Sport treibst du gern?
Which sport do you like?

das Angeln ....fishing
der Basketball ....basketball

das Badminton..............badminton
der Fußball ....football
das Golf ....golf
die Gymnastik ....gymnastics
das Hockey ....hockey
das Jogging...................jogging
das Kricket ....cricket
die Leichtathletik ....athletics
der Netzball ....netball
das Radfahren...............cycling
das Reiten ....horse riding
das Rugby.....................rugby
das Schwimmen ....swimming
das Tennis.....................tennis
das Tischtennis ....table tennis
der Volleyball...............volleyball

der Boxsport.................boxing
das Darts.......................darts
das Drachenfliegen ....hang gliding
der Handball.................handball
der Hochsprung ....high jump
das Judo........................judo
die Kampfsportarten *pl* ..... martial arts
das Kegeln ....bowling
der Korbball ....netball
das Rollschuhlaufen ......roller skating
das Schlittschuhlaufen.. ice skating
das Segeln.....................sailing
das Skilaufen ....ski-ing
das Snooker ....snooker
der Wassersport............water sports
der Weitsprung.............long jump
das Windsurfen.............wind surfing
der Wintersport ....winter sports

Die Sportausrüstung   Sports equipment
der Badeanzug (-züge) . swimsuit
der Ball (Bälle).............ball
der Fußball (-bälle).......football

die Fußballschuhe *pl* .... football boots
der Hockeyschläger (-) .... hockey stick
der Kricketschläger (-) .... cricket bat
das Mountainbike (s) ... mountain bike
die Rollschuhe *pl* .... roller skates
der Ski (s) .... ski
das Surfbrett (er) .... surfboard
der Tennisschläger (-) .. tennis racket
die Turnschuhe *pl* .... trainers (shoes)

Wie ist es?   What is it like?
amüsant .... funny
andere .... other
anstrengend .... tiring
astrein *coll* .... great, super
aufregend .... exciting
beliebt .... popular
echt .... real
eindrucksvoll .... impressive
einmalig .... great, brilliant
energisch .... energetic
nicht gestattet .... not allowed
nutzlos .... useless
nicht schlecht .... not bad
schrecklich .... awful
sportlich .... sporty, keen on sport
super .... super

Was machst du?   What do you do?
gewinnen *irreg* .... to win
schwimmen (*) *irreg* ... to swim
spazieren gehen* *irreg* to go for a walk
Fußball spielen .... to play football
Sport treiben *irreg* .... to do sport
verlieren *irreg* .... to lose
wandern* .... to hike, go for a long walk

Rad fahren* *irreg* .... to cycle
Rollschuh fahren* .... to roller-skate
Skateboard fahren* ...... to skateboard
Ski fahren* .... to ski

angeln gehen* *irreg* ..... to go fishing

sich anmelden † *sep* ..... to enrol
ausrüsten † *sep* .... to equip
fangen *irreg* .... to catch (fish)
Schlittschuh laufen* *irreg* .. to skate
eine Radtour machen .... to go cycling
reiten* *irreg* .... to go horse riding
ein Tor schießen *irreg* .. to score a goal
segeln .... to go sailing
springen* *irreg* .... to jump, leap
teilnehmen *irreg sep* ..... to participate
unterstützen † *insep* ...... to support
verteidigen † .... to defend
werfen *irreg* .... to throw
windsurfen .... to windsurf

In die Stadt gehen Going into town
mit dem Auto .... by car
mit dem Bus .... by bus
mit dem Rad .... on a bicycle
mit dem Taxi .... by taxi
mit dem Wagen .... by car
mit dem Zug .... by train

mit der Bahn .... by train
mit der Straßenbahn ..... by tram
mit der U-Bahn .... on the underground
zu Fuß .... on foot

der Bahnhof (-höfe) ...... station
der Busbahnhof (-höfe) ..... bus station
die Bushaltestelle (n) .... bus stop
die Buslinie (n) .... bus route
die einfache Fahrkarte .. single ticket
die Endstation (en) .... terminus
der Fahrkartenautomat (en) *wk*
.... ticket machine
der Fahrkartenschalter (-) ..... ticket office
der Fahrplan (-pläne) .... timetable
die Hauptverkehrszeit (en) ... rush hour
die Rückfahrkarte (n) .... return ticket
die Straßenbahnhaltestelle (n) .. tram stop
die Straßenbahnlinie (n) .... tram line

die U-Bahnstation (en) ....underground station
die Verbindung (en) ....connection
das Verkehrsamt (-ämter) .....tourist office

direkt............................direct, through
gültig............................valid
letzt ....last
nächst............................next

Wo gehst du hin?   Where do you go?
der Ball (Bälle) ....ball
die Disco (s) ....disco
der Jugendklub (s) ....youth club
das Jugendzentrum (-zentren)... youth centre
das Kino (s)..................cinema
der Nachtklub (s)..........night club
die Party (s) ....party (celebration)
der Tanz (Tänze) ....dance

die Eisbahn (en)............ice rink
das Freibad (-bäder)......open air pool
das Hallenbad (-bäder)..indoor swimming pool
die Kegelbahn (en) ....bowling alley
das Schwimmbad (-bäder) ..... swimming pool
der Sportplatz (-plätze).......... sports ground
das Sportzentrum (-zentren) .. sports centre
das Stadion (Stadien)....stadium
der Verein (e)................club, society

der Ausflug (-flüge)......trip, outing
die Ausstellung (en) .....exhibition
die Führung (en)..........guided tour
die Halle (n).................hall (public, sport)
das Konzert (e).............concert
die Galerie (n) ....art gallery
das Theater (-)..............theatre
der Tiergarten (-gärten) .....zoo
das Treffen (-)..............meeting

einkaufen gehen* *irreg.*to go shopping
einen Einkaufsbummel machen
................................to go round the shops

einen Schaufensterbummel machen
...............................to go window shopping
Schlange stehen *irreg*...to queue
besuchen †...................to visit
in die Stadt gehen* *irreg*.. to go to town
nach Hause kommen* *irreg*
...............................to come back home
mitfahren* *irreg sep*..... to go with s.o
sich treffen *irreg* ....to meet
das Haus verlassen *irreg*.. to leave the house

entwerten †...................to date-stamp ticket
Fotos machen ....to take photos
einen Platz reservieren † .. to book a seat
ein Schloss besuchen † ..... to look round a
                              stately home/castle

zum Gottesdienst gehen* *irreg*
......................to go to (protestant) church
zur Messe gehen*.........to go to mass
zur Moschee gehen* ....to go to the mosque
zur Synagoge gehen* ..to go to the synagogue

For **transport** see page 27
For **times** see page 86

Die Musik   Music
die CD (s)....................CD
die Kassette (n) ....cassette
die Stereoanlage (n) .....stereo system
der Walkman® (s)........personal stereo

die Blockflöte (n)........recorder
die Geige (n) ....violin
die Gitarre (n)..............guitar
das Instrument (e)........instrument
das Keyboard (s)..........keyboard
die Klarinette (n)..........clarinet
das Klavier (e)..............piano (upright)
die Posaune (n) ....trombone
die Querflöte (n)..........flute
das Schlagzeug ....drum kit
die Trompete (n) ....trumpet

die Art (en) .... type, sort
die Band (s) .... group
der Chor (Chöre)......... choir
der Hit (s).................... hit song (in English)
das Lied (er) .... song
das Orchester (-)........... orchestra, band
der Schlager (-) .... hit song (in German)

leise............................. quietly
laut .... loudly

Popmusik hören .... to listen to pop music
Rockmusik hören......... to listen to rock music
musizieren † .... to make music
im Chor singen *irreg* ... to sing in the choir
klassische Musik spielen
.... to play classical music
Klavier spielen............. to play the piano
Schlagzeug spielen ...... to play the drums
üben .... to practise

Zu Hause bleiben   Staying at home

das Basteln .... model-making
das Damespiel .... draughts
die DVD (s) .... DVD
der Film (e) .... film
der Fotoapparat (e)....... camera
das Fotografieren .... photography
die Freizeitbeschäftigung...hobby
das Gesellschaftsspiel (e)...board game
das Hobby (s) .... hobby
die Illustrierte (n) ‡ magazine
die Karten *pl* .... cards
das Kochen.................. cooking
das Kreuzworträtsel (-) crossword
der Kriminalroman (e) . detective story
die Lektüre.................. reading
das Malen.................... painting
die Musik.................... music
das Nähen................... sewing
das Poster (-) .... poster
der Roman (e) .... novel

die Sammlung (en)....... collection
das Schach .... chess
der Science-Fiction-Roman (e)
.... sci-fi story
das Video.................... video
das Zeichnen............... drawing
die Zeitschrift (en)....... magazine

sich amüsieren † .... to amuse o.s
sich ausruhen *sep* .... to rest
basteln .... to make models, do DIY
einen Film drehen........ to make a film
sich entspannen † .... to relax
faulenzen † .... to laze about
fernsehen *irreg sep*....... to watch TV
sich interessieren für † (+ Acc)
.... to be interested in
malen.......................... to paint
modellieren †............... to make models
nähen .... to sew
sammeln .... to collect
Karten spielen .... to play cards
stricken .... to knit
zeichnen † .... to draw

Informatik   ICT

der Bildschirm (e) .... screen, monitor
der CD ROM (s).......... CD ROM
der Chip (s).................. chip
der Computer (-).......... computer
die Computermusik...... computer music
das Computerspiel (e)...computer game
der Cursor (s)............... cursor
die Datei (en)............... data-base, file
der Diskmanager (-) ..... disk manager
der Diskdrive (s).......... disk drive
die Diskette (n)........... disk
der Drucker (-)............. printer
die E-Mail (s) .... e-mail
die Festplatte (n) .... hard disk
das Internet .... internet
der Joystick (s) .... joystick

die Maus (Mäuse).........mouse
das Menü (s) ....menu
die Software ....computer software
die Tastatur (en) ....keyboard
die Textverarbeitung ....word processing
das Videospiel (e) ....video game
die Website (s)..............web site

elektrisch ....electrical
elektronisch ....electronic
technisch......................technical
technologisch...............technological

aufmachen *sep*..............to open
bearbeiten †..................to edit
drucken.........................to print
formatieren † ....to format
klicken..........................to click
laden *irreg*...................to load
programmieren † ....to program
speichern ....to save
tippen ....to type

For **Saturday jobs** see page 56
For **'when, where, with whom'** see page 32
For **opinions** see page 78

1C HOME AND LOCAL ENVIRONMENT

Die Adresse   Address

die Adresse (n)............. address
die E-Mail-Adresse...... e-mail address
die Faxnummer (n)...... fax number
die Nummer (n).......... number
die Postleitzahl (en)..... postcode
die Telefonnummer (n) phone number
der Wohnort (e).......... place of residence

die Allee (n)................. avenue
die Brücke (n)............. bridge
die Gasse (n)............... passage, alley
die Hauptstraße (n)...... main road
der Kai (s)................... embankment, quay
der Platz (Plätze).......... square
die Sackgasse (n)........ cul de sac
die Straße (n).............. street, road
der Weg (e)................. lane, path, way
der Wohnort (e) .... place of residence
das Zentrum (Zentren) . centre

Die Gegend   Situation

das Dorf (Dörfer) .... village
der Kreis (e)................ county
das Land (Länder) .... region; country; state
das Meer (e) .... sea
die See (n).................. sea
die Stadt (Städte) .... town
das Viertel (-) .... district of town, city
der Vorort (e) .... suburb

auf dem Land................in the country
in der Stadt ....in the town
im Norden ....in the north
im Osten ....in the east
im Süden ....in the south
im Westen ....in the west

nördlich von (+ Dat).....north of
östlich von (+ Dat) ....east of
südlich von (+ Dat) ......south of
westlich von (+ Dat).....west of

Häuser   Housing

der Bauernhof (-höfe)...farm
der Bungalow (s) ....bungalow
das Doppelhaus (-häuser) . semi-detached house
das Einfamilienhaus (-häuser) .. detached house
das Gebäude (n)...........building
das Haus (Häuser) ....house
das Hochhaus (-häuser) ... tower block
das Reihenhaus (-häuser). terraced house
die Sozialwohnung (en) .. housing association flat
das Studio (s)...............bedsit
der Wohnblock (s)........block of flats
die Wohnung (en) ....flat

der Besitzer (-)..............owner
der Einwohner (-) ....inhabitant
die Miete (n)................rent
der Mieter (-) ....tenant
der Umzug..................house move

Phrases

Wo wohnst du? *Where do you live?*   Ich wohne in Malvern *I live in Malvern*

Ich wohne im ersten Stock *I live on the first floor*

Welche Zimmer gibt es bei dir zu Hause? *What rooms are there in your house?*

Es gibt drei Schlafzimmer, eine Küche, ein Esszimmer, ein Wohnzimmer und ein Badezimmer.
There are three bedrooms, a kitchen, a dining room, a living room and a bathroom

Allgemeines	**General**
der Aufzug (-züge)	lift
der Eingang (-gänge)	entrance
der Fahrstuhl (-stühle)	lift
der Flur (e)	hall
der Gang (Gänge)	corridor
die Haustür (e)	(front) door
der Lift (s)	lift
der Plan (Pläne)	plan
der Stock (-)	floor, storey
die Treppe (n)	staircase
der Treppenflur (e)	landing

im Erdgeschoss	on the ground floor
im Keller	in the cellar
im ersten Stock	on the first floor
oben	upstairs
unten	downstairs

Die Zimmer   Rooms

das Arbeitszimmer (-)	study
das Badezimmer (-)	bathroom
der Dachboden (-böden)	attic, loft
die Diele (n)	hall
das Esszimmer (-)	dining room
die Garage (n)	garage
der Hausflur (e)	hall
der Keller (-)	cellar, basement
das Kinderzimmer (-)	playroom
das Klo (s)	toilet, loo
die Küche (n)	kitchen
das Schlafzimmer (-)	bedroom
der Speicher (-)	attic, loft
die Toilette (n)	toilet
die Waschküche (n)	utility room

der Wintergarten (-gärten)	conservatory
das Wohnzimmer (-)	living-room, lounge

Das Schlafzimmer   Bedroom

das Bett (en)	bed
das Buch (Bücher)	book
die Gardine (n)	net curtain
die Haarbürste (n)	brush
der Kamm (Kämme)	comb
die Kassette (n)	cassette
der Kleiderschrank (-schränke)	wardrobe
die Kommode (n)	chest of drawers
die Lampe (n)	lamp
das Poster (-)	poster
das Regal (e)	shelf
der Schreibtisch (e)	desk
die Schublade (n)	drawer
der Sessel (-)	easy chair
der Spiegel (-)	mirror
der Stuhl (Stühle)	chair (hard)
der Teppich (e)	rug, carpet (not fitted)
der Teppichboden (böden)	fitted carpet
der Vorhang (-hänge)	curtain
der Walkman® (s)	personal stereo
der Wecker (-)	alarm clock
eigen	own, private

die CD (s)	CD
der Computer (-)	computer
der Fernseher (-)	TV set
der Föhn (e)	hairdryer
der Radiowecker (-)	radio clock
das Spielzeug *no pl*	toys
die Stereoanlage (n)	stereo system
das Videospiel (e)	video game

Phrases

Teilst du dein Zimmer? *Do you share a room?*

Nein, ich habe mein eigenes Zimmer *No, I have my own room*

Ja, ich teile mit meinem Bruder/meiner Schwester *Yes, I share with my brother/sister*

Was gibt es in deinem Schlafzimmer? *What is there in your bedroom?*

In meinem Zimmer habe ich ein Bett, einen Tisch, einen Computer und eine Lampe *I have a bed, a table, a computer and a lamp in my room*

Die Küche	**Kitchen**
der Elektroherd (e).......	electric cooker
der Gasherd (e)	gas cooker
der Kühlschrank (-schränke)..	fridge
der Mikrowellenherd (e)...microwave (oven)	
der Ofen (Öfen)	oven
die Spülmaschine (n)...	dishwasher
die Tiefkühltruhe (n) ...	freezer
die Waschmaschine (n)	washing machine
tiefgefroren	deep frozen
das Bügeleisen (-)	iron
der Schrank (Schränke)	cupboard
das Spülbecken (-)	sink
der Staubsauger (-).......	vacuum cleaner
die Trockenschleuder (n)...spin dryer	
der Wäschetrockner (-)	tumble dryer
der Toaster (-)	toaster
der Abfalleimer (-).......	rubbish bin
die Bratpfanne (n)........	frying pan
das Bügelbrett (er)........	ironing board
der Dosenöffner (-)	can opener
der Flaschenöffner (-) ..	bottle opener
das Geschirrtuch (-tücher)...	tea towel
die Streichhölzer *pl*......	matches
das Tablett (s)..............	tray
das Telefon (e)	telephone
der Topf (Töpfe)	saucepan
das Waschpulver	washing powder

Das Esszimmer	**Dining room**
die Anrichte (n)...........	sideboard
das Gemälde (-)	painting
die Kerze (n)	candle
der Stuhl (Stühle)	chair
der Tisch (e)	table
die Tischdecke (n).......	tablecloth

Das Wohnzimmer	**Living room, Lounge**
der Aschenbecher (-)....ashtray	
das Bücherregal (e).......	book-case
der CD-Spieler (-)	CD player
der Couchtisch (e)	coffee table
der DVD-Spieler (-)	DVD player
der Fernseher (-)..........	TV set
das Foto (s)	photo
der Kamin (e)	fireplace
der Kassettenrekorder (-)..	cassette recorder
das Kissen (-)...............	cushion
das Klavier (e)	piano
der Sessel (-)................	armchair
das Sofa (s)	sofa, settee
die Stereoanlage (-)	stereo system
der Teppichboden (-böden) ...	fitted carpet
die Uhr (en)	clock
die Vase (n)	vase
der Videorekorder (-) ...	video recorder

Das Badezimmer	**Bathroom**
das Bad	bath (activity)
das Badetuch (-tücher)..	bath towel
die Badewanne (e)........	bath (tub)

14

das Bidet (s) .... bidet
das Deo (s) .... deodorant
die Dusche (n) .... shower
das Handtuch (-tücher) .towel
der Rasierapparat (e)..... razor
das Schaumbad .... bubble bath
der Schwamm (Schwämme).. sponge
die Seife........................ soap
das Shampoo (s)............ shampoo
der Spiegel (-).............. mirror
das Toilettenpapier .... toilet paper
das Waschbecken (-)..... wash basin
der Waschlappen (-) ..... flannel
der Wasserhahn (-hähne).. tap
die Zahnbürste (n) .... toothbrush
die Zahnpasta .... toothpaste
    heißes Wasser .... hot water
    kaltes Wasser .... cold water

For **helping at home** see page 50
For **daily routine** see page 20

Allgemeines   General

der Anstrich .... paint(ing)
die Aussicht (en) .... view
der Balkon (s) .... balcony
das Dach (Dächer) .... roof
die Decke (n) .... ceiling
der Dekor .... décor
das Fenster (-) .... window
der Fußboden (-böden) . floor
die Gartenpforte (n)...... gate
das Glas........................ glass
der Griff (e) .... handle
die Klingel (n) .... doorbell
die Mauer (n)............... wall (external)
die Möbel *pl* .... furniture
der Quadratmeter (-)..... square metre
der Rollladen (-läden)... shutter
das Schloss (Schlösser).... lock
die Tapete (n) .... wallpaper
die Wand (Wände) .... wall (internal)
das Gas........................ gas

die Glühbirne (n).......... light bulb
der Heizkörper (-)........ radiator
das Kabel (-)................ flex
das Licht (er) .... light
das Putzen................... cleaning
der Schalter (-) .... switch
die Steckdose (n)......... plug
der Strom..................... electricity, current
das Wasser................... water
die Zentralheizung .... central heating

Die Garage   Garage

das Auto (s) .... car
das Fahrrad (-räder)...... bike
das Motorrad (-räder) ... motorbike
der Rasenmäher (-)....... lawnmower
der Roller (-) .... scooter
der Wagen (-) .... car
das Werkzeug *no pl* ...... tools

Der Garten   Garden

der Apfelbaum (-bäume).. apple tree
der Baum (Bäume) .... tree
die Blume (n) .... flower
das Blumenbeet (e)....... flower bed
der Busch (Büsche) ...... bush
das Gemüse .... vegetable
der Gemüsegarten (-gärten)....vegetable garden
die Gemüsesorte (n).............type of vegetable
das Gewächshaus (-häuser) ....greenhouse
das Gras....................... grass
das Obst....................... fruit
der Obstbaum (-bäume) .... fruit tree
die Obstsorte (n) .... type of fruit
die Pflanze (n)............. plant
der Rasen (-)................ lawn
die Rose (n)................. rose
der Schuppen (-).......... shed
die Tanne (n)............... fir tree
die Terrasse (n) .... patio, terrace

Wie ist das Haus?	**What is it like?**
bequem	comfortable
elegant.........................	elegant
eng	cramped
freundlich....................	welcoming
gemütlich	cosy
hübsch.........................	pretty
leer	empty
luxuriös.......................	luxurious
möbliert	furnished
nagelneu......................	brand new
notwendig	necessary
perfekt.........................	perfect
praktisch	practical
schick..........................	smart
seltsam	odd, strange
unentbehrlich	essential
vornehm......................	posh

in gutem Zustand	in good condition
in schlechtem Zustand .	in poor condition

ehemalig	ex-, former
industriell....................	industrial
malerisch.....................	picturesque
touristisch	tourist
typisch.........................	typical

Wo ist es?	**Where is it?**
im Erdgeschoss............	on the ground floor
im ersten Stock	on the first floor
unten	downstairs
oben	upstairs
hinter dem Haus...........	behind the house
vor dem Haus...............	in front of the house
mit Blick auf den Garten	
....	overlooking the garden
mit Blick auf die Straße	
....	overlooking the street

Umgebung	**Geography**
der Bach (Bäche).........	stream
der Berg (e).................	mountain
die Entfernung (en)	distance
der Fluss (Flüsse)	river
das Gebiet (e)...............	region
das Gebirge (-)..............	mountain range
die Höhle (n)	cave
der Hügel (-).................	hill
die Insel (n)	island
das Klima (s)	climate
das Land (Länder)........	country; countryside
die Provinz (en)...........	province
die See (n)	sea
der See (n)	lake
das Tal (Täler)	valley

das Dorf (Dörfer)..........	village
die Grenze (n)	border
die Großstadt (-städte)..	city
die Hauptstadt (-städte)	capital
die Industrie (n)...........	industry
die Landwirtschaft.......	agriculture
der Lärm	noise
die Stadt (Städte).........	town
der Vorort (e)...............	suburb

Leute	**People**
der Autofahrer (-)	motorist
der Bauer (n) *wk*	farmer
die Bäuerin (nen).........	female farmer
der Fußgänger (-)..........	pedestrian
der Landwirt (en).........	farmer
die Menge (n)	crowd
der Polizist (en) *wk*.......	policeman
die Polizistin (nen).......	policewoman
der Radfahrer (-)..........	cyclist
der Stadtbewohner (-)...	city dweller

In der Stadt   In town

Gebäude   Buildings

der Bahnhof (-höfe) ......station
die Bank (en) ....bank
die Bibliothek (en)........library
das Büro (s)...................office
das Einkaufszentrum (-zentren)
   ....shopping centre
die Fabrik (en) ....factory
das Geschäft (e) ....shop
der Jugendklub (s) ....youth club
das Kino (s)...................cinema
die Kirche (n) ....church
das Krankenhaus (-häuser) .... hospital
der Laden (Läden) ....shop
der Markt (Märkte).......market
das Parkhaus (-häuser)..multi-storey car park
der Parkplatz (-plätze) ..car park
die Post ....post office
das Postamt (-ämter) .....post office
das Rathaus (-häuser)....town hall
die Schule (-n) ....school
das Schwimmbad (-bäder) .. swimming pool
die Sparkasse (n) ....bank
die Tankstelle (n).........petrol station

die Burg (en)................castle (fortified)

der Campingplatz (-plätze) ....campsite
der Dom (e) ....cathedral
das Hotel (s) ....hotel
das Informationsbüro (s) .. tourist office
das Museum (Museen) ...... museum
das Schloss (Schlösser) ..... stately home, castle
das Stadion (Stadien).... stadium
das Theater (-) ....theatre
der Turm (Türme) ....tower
das Verkehrsamt (-ämter).. tourist office

die Altstadt .... town centre
der Busbahnhof (-höfe) ..... bus station
die Eisbahn (en) ....ice rink
der Flughafen (-häfen).. airport
die Innenstadt...............town centre
die Jugendherberge (n). youth hostel
die Klinik (en).............. clinic, hospital
der Park (s)................... park
das Polizeirevier (e)...... police station
die Polizeiwache (n) .... police station
das Reisebüro (s) .... travel agency
das Sportzentrum (-zentren)...sports centre
die Stadtmitte (n) .... town centre
die Telefonzelle (n)......phone box
der Wohnblock (s)........ block of flats
der Zeitungskiosk (e) ... newspaper stand

Phrases

Ich wohne seit zehn Jahren in Malvern *I have lived in Malvern for ten years*

Malvern ist eine Kleinstadt in der Nähe von Worcester *Malvern is a small town near Worcester*

Was gibt es in Malvern zu sehen? *What is there to see in Malvern?*

Es gibt die Berge, ein kleines Museum, einen Park und eine große Kirche *There are the hills, a small museum, a park and a big church*

Man kann ins Theater, ins Kino oder ins Hallenbad gehen *You can go to the theatre, the cinema or the swimming pool*

Man kann auf den Bergen spazieren gehen *You can go for walks on the hills*

17

Orientierungspunkte Landmarks
die Allee (n)............... avenue (with trees)
die Ampel.................. traffic lights,
                            pelican crossing
die Autobahn (en)........ motorway
der Briefkasten (-kästen).......letter box
die Brücke (n)............. bridge
die Bushaltestelle (n)... bus stop
die Ecke (n)................ corner
die Kreuzung (en)........ crossroads
der Marktplatz (-plätze)market square
der Platz (Plätze).......... square
die Straßenecke (n)...... corner of the road
die U-Bahn .... underground

der Bahnübergang (-gänge)..level crossing
die Baustelle (n).......... roadworks
der Bürgersteig (e)....... pavement
das Denkmal (-mäler) .. monument
die Fußgängerzone (n). pedestrian zone
der Hafen (Häfen)........ port
die Unterführung (en).. subway
der Verkehr................ traffic
der Verkehrskreisel...... roundabout
der Zebrastreifen (-)..... pedestrian crossing

die Graffiti *pl* .... graffiti
der Kirchturm (-türme) church tower
der Stadtteil (e) .... part of a town
das Straßenschild (er)... road sign
die Umgehungsstraße (n)..ring road, bypass

Im Park   In the park
die Bank (Bänke)........ bench
die Blume (n).............. flower
das Blumenbeet (e) ...... flower bed
der Brunnen (-) .... fountain
der Kinderspielplatz (-plätze) .....play area
die Schaukel (n).......... swing
die Wiese (n) .... grassed area

Auf dem Land   In the country
der Baum (Bäume) ....tree
das Feld (er)................field (arable)
das Ferienhaus (-häuser)... holiday cottage
der Fluss (Flüsse) ....river
der Gipfel (-) ....summit
das Gras ....grass
die Hecke (n)...............hedge
der Hof (Höfe).............yard
der Hügel (-)................hill
die Kapelle (n).............chapel
das Land......................countryside
die Landschaft (en).......countryside, scenery
die Natur.....................nature
das Ufer (-) ....riverbank
der Wald (Wälder)........forest, wood
der Wanderweg (e).......footpath
die Wiese (n)...............field (pasture)

Auf dem Bauernhof   On the farm
das Bauernhaus (-häuser) . farmhouse
der Bauernhof (-höfe)...farm
die Ernte (n) ....harvest
die Hühner *pl*...............hens
die Kuh (Kühe)............cow
das Schaf (e) ....sheep
das Schwein (e) ....pig
der Stall (Ställe)...........stable
der Traktor (en) ....tractor
der Weinbauer (n) *wk*...wine grower
der Weingarten (-gärten) .. vineyard

Wie ist es?   What is it like?
benachbart ....nearby, neighbouring
breit ....wide
entzückend ....charming
flach...........................flat
gefährlich....................dangerous
historisch ....historic
malerisch ....picturesque
mehrere.......................several
in der Nähe ....near

18

natürlich........................natural
örtlich ....local
still...............................peaceful
verschmutzt ....polluted
wild..............................wild
umgeben von (+ Dat)....surrounded by

For **prepositions** see page 80
For **weather** see page 33

Nützliche Verben　　**Useful verbs**
sich befinden *irreg* ....to be situated
bis ... gehen* *irreg* ....to go as far as
überqueren *insep* ....to cross
an (+ Dat) vorbeigehen* *irreg sep*
.... to go past
weiterfahren* *irreg sep* .. to drive on, continue
weitergehen* *irreg sep*... to walk on, continue

Phrases – My home town

Vorteile *Advantages*

Es gibt viel zu tun. Im Stadtzentrum gibt es Kinos und viele Geschäfte
There's lots to do. There are cinemas and lots of shops in the town centre

Alle zehn Minuten gibt es einen Bus *Buses run every ten minutes*

Es gibt ein Hallenbad und ein großes Sportzentrum *There is a swimming pool and a big sports centre*

Nachteile *Disadvantages*

Es gibt nichts für Jugendliche zu tun *There is nothing for teenagers to do*

Es gibt nur ein paar Geschäfte und das Kino ist klein *There are only a few shops and the cinema is small*

Es gibt weder Busse noch ein Sportzentrum *There are no buses and there isn't a sports centre*

Es ist langweilig *It's boring*

1D DAILY ROUTINE

in der Schule ankommen* *irreg sep*
.... to arrive at school
sich anziehen *irreg sep* to get dressed
sich fein anziehen .... to dress smartly
aufstehen* *irreg sep* .... to get up
aufwachen* *sep* .... to wake up
sich ausziehen *irreg sep*.....to get undressed
sich duschen................ to shower
zu Abend essen *irreg*... to have evening meal
zu Mittag essen *irreg*... to have lunch
frühstücken .... to have breakfast
ins Bett gehen* *irreg* ... to go to bed
Hausaufgaben machen ....to do homework
das Haus verlassen *irreg*....to leave the house
sich waschen *irreg*....... to get washed

ausschlafen *irreg sep* ... to have a lie in
sich beeilen † .... to rush
sich die Haare bürsten † ....to brush one's hair
einschlafen* *irreg sep*.. to fall asleep
in die Stadt gehen* *irreg* ...to go into town
sich hinlegen *sep*......... to lie down
sich kämmen .... to comb one's hair
sich die Zähne putzen † ... to clean one's teeth
sich rasieren † .... to shave
sich schminken .... to put on make-up

Sport treiben *irreg*......... to do sport
sich die Haare trocknen † ..to dry one's hair
sich umziehen *irreg sep* ....to get changed
wecken ....to wake s.o

Die Schuluniform School uniform

die Bluse (n)................blouse
das Hemd (en) ....shirt
die Hose (n).................trousers
die Jacke (n) ....blazer
das Kleid (er) ....dress
der Pulli (s)..................pullover
der Pullover (-) ....pullover
der Rock (Röcke) ....skirt
der Schlips (e) ....tie
der Schuh (e) ....shoe
die Socke (n) ....sock
die Strumpfhose (n)......tights
die Wolljacke (n).........cardigan

altmodisch ....old-fashioned
praktisch ....practical

For **food** see page 52
For **going into town** see page 8

Phrases

Um halb acht wache ich auf *I wake up at 7.30*

Ich stehe auf, wasche mich, dusche mich, ziehe mich an *I get up, wash, shower, get dressed*

Ich putze mir die Zähne, ich bürste mir die Haare *I clean my teeth, I brush my hair*

Ich frühstücke *I have breakfast*

Um Viertel nach acht verlasse ich das Haus und ich komme um Viertel vor neun in der Schule an
   I leave the house at 8.15 and I arrive at school at 8.45

Zu Mittag esse ich in der Schule *I have lunch at school*

Um halb fünf komme ich zu Hause an und ich mache meine Hausaufgaben *I get home at 4.30
   and I do my homework*

Um halb elf gehe ich ins Bett *I go to bed at 10.30*

1E SCHOOL AND FUTURE PLANS

Der Schulbesuch   School attendance

die Schule (n) ....(state) school
die Ganztagsschule (n) .all-day school
die Gesamtschule (n)....comprehensive school
die Grundschule (n)......primary school
das Gymnasium (Gymnasien)... grammar school
die Hauptschule (n) ......secondary modern
das Internat (e) ....boarding school
der Kindergarten (-gärten) .... nursery school
das Oberstufenkolleg (-kollegien)
      .... sixth form/tertiary college
die private Grundschule (n)...... prep school
die Privatschule (n) ......public school

die Realschule (n) ....secondary school type
die Berufsschule.......... Technical College
die Universität (en) ...... university

in der 6. Klasse............. in Year 7
in der 7. Klasse............. in Year 8
in der 8. Klasse............. in Year 9
in der 9. Klasse............. in Year 10
in der 10. Klasse........... in Year 11
in der 11. Klasse........... in Year 12
in der 12. Klasse........... in Year 13
in der Oberstufe............ in the Sixth Form

Phrases

Wie viele Schüler und Schülerinnen gibt es in deiner Schule? *How many pupils are there in your school?*

In unserer Schule gibt es tausend Schüler und Schülerinnen *There are 1,000 pupils in our school*

Wie viele gibt es in deiner Klasse? *How many are there in your class?*

Wir sind siebenundzwanzig in der Klasse *There are 27 in my class*

Wo befindet sich deine Schule? *Where is your school?*

In der Stadtmitte/In einem Vorort *In the town centre/in a suburb*

Wir haben fünf Informatikräume und einen großen Sportplatz
    There are 5 ICT rooms and a big sports field

Leute   People

der Abiturient (en) *wk*...sixth former
die Abiturientin (nen)...sixth former
der Internatsschüler (-) .boarder
der Klassenkamerad (en) *wk*.. classmate
die Klassenkameradin (nen).. classmate
der Klassensprecher (-)......class spokesperson
der Schüler (-)..............school student
die Schülerin (nen) ....school student
der Schulfreund (e).......school friend
die Schulfreundin (nen).....school friend
der Tagesschüler (-)......day-pupil

der Berufsberater (-).....careers officer
der Direktor (en)...........headmaster
die Direktorin (nen) .....headmistress
der Hausmeister (-).......caretaker
der Lehrer (-)................teacher
die Lehrerin (nen) ....teacher
der Schulleiter (-) ....head
die Sekretärin (nen)......secretary
die SMV......................school council
der Sprachassistent (en) *wk*.. language assistant
der Studienrat (-räte) ....secondary teacher
die Studienrätin (nen) ..secondary teacher
der Inspektor (en).........inspector

Das Schulgebäude
The school complex

der Arbeitsraum (-räume) ..private study room
die Aula (Aulen).......... school hall
die Bibliothek (en)....... library
das schwarze Brett .... notice board
das Büro (s)................. office
der Fußballplatz (-plätze).... football pitch
der Gang (Gänge) .... corridor
die Kantine (n)............. canteen
das Klassenzimmer (-) . classroom
das Labor (s) .... laboratory
das Lazarett (e)............. sick bay
das Lehrerzimmer (-) ... staffroom
der Lehrmittelraum (-räume) . resources centre
das Schwimmbad (-bäder) ..... swimming pool
der Schlafraum (-räume)........ dormitory
der Schulhof (-höfe).............. playground
das Sprachlabor (s)................ language lab
der Tennisplatz (-plätze)........ tennis court
die Turnhalle (n)................... gym
der Umkleideraum (-räume) .. changing room
der Werkraum (-räume) .... workshop, studio

aus Backstein .... of brick
aus Beton .... of concrete
gemischt...................... mixed

Die Fächer   School subjects

das Fach (Fächer)......... subject
die Fremdsprache (n)... foreign language
das Lieblingsfach (-fächer) .... favourite subject
die Naturwissenschaft (en) .... science
das Pflichtfach (-fächer).....compulsory subject
das Wahlfach (-fächer).......optional subject

Biologie....................... biology
Chemie .... chemistry
Deutsch........................ German
Englisch........................ English
Erdkunde .... geography
Französisch.................. French
Geographie .... geography
Geschichte................... history
Kunst ....art
Mathe(matik)............... maths, mathematics
Musik .... music
Physik .... physics
Religion(slehre)............ RE
Spanisch .... Spanish
Sport .... PE
Technologie................. technology

Betriebswirtschaft .... business studies
Drama........................... Expressive Arts
Handarbeit .... needlework
Hauswirtschaftslehre .... domestic science
Informatik................... ICT, computer studies
Kochen .... cookery
Latein........................... Latin
Medienwissenschaft ..... media studies
Sozialkunde................. social science
Turnen .... gymnastics
Werken .... CDT
Wirtschaftslehre .... economics

Phrases

Mein Lieblingsfach ist Geographie *My favourite lesson is geography*
Ich bin gut/schwach in Geschichte *I am good/poor at history*
Ich bekomme immer schlechte Noten in Französisch *I always get bad marks in French*

Der Schultag   **The school day**
die Hausaufgaben *pl*.....homework, prep
das Mittagessen (-)........midday meal
die Mittagspause (n).....dinner hour
der Morgen (-) ....morning
der Nachmittag (e)........afternoon
die Pause (n).................break
der Schulschluss ....end of school day
die Stunde (n)...............lesson
die Versammlung (en)..assembly

aufpassen † *sep*
.......................to be careful, pay attention
die Anwesenheit feststellen *sep*
.............................to call the register
ruhig sein* *irreg*..........to be quiet
sich setzen † ....to sit down
eine Frage stellen ....to ask a question

For **school uniform** see page 20
For **times** see page 86

Phrases

Der Unterricht beginnt um neun Uhr und ist um vier Uhr zu Ende *Lessons start at 9 and end at 4*
Die Mittagspause ist von halb eins bis halb zwei *Lunch break is from 12.30 to 1.30*
Ich komme mit dem Auto/mit dem Bus/mit dem Rad zur Schule *I come to school by car/by bus/by bike*
Ich komme zu Fuß zur Schule *I walk to school*
Ich bin Mitglied in der Hockeymannschaft *I'm in the hockey team*

Das Schuljahr   **The school year**

die Ferien *pl*.................holiday
die Halbjahresferien .....February half term
die Herbstferien............autumn half term
die Osterferien ....Easter holiday
die Pfingstferien ....summer half term
der Schüleraustausch ....school exchange
das Semester (-) ....semester
die Sommerferien *pl*.....summer holidays
der Stundenplan (-pläne) ..timetable
der freie Tag ....day off
das Trimester (-) ....term
der Unterricht ....teaching
die Weihnachtsferien....Christmas holidays
die Woche (n)..............week
hitzefrei.......................day off due to heat

Im Klassenzimmer   **In the classroom**
das Fach (Fächer)..........locker, pigeon hole
das Fenster (-) ....window

die Kreide....................chalk
der Lehrertisch (e) ....teacher's desk
der Schrank (Schränke).....cupboard
der Stuhl (Stühle) ....chair
die Tafel (n) ....(black/white) board
der Tisch (e) ....table
die Tür (en) ....door

der Bildschirm (e) ....screen
der Computer (-) ....computer
der Kassettenrekorder (-) . tape recorder
der Kopfhörer..............headset
das Mikrophon (e)........microphone
der Schwamm (Schwämme) ..sponge
der Tageslichtprojektor (en)
.... overhead projector
der Videorekorder (-) ... video recorder

die Aufgabe (n) ....exercise
der Aufsatz (-sätze) ......essay
der Auszug (-züge).......extract

der Bericht (e)............. report (of event)
die Grammatik............ grammar
die Klassenarbeit (en).. assessment/class test
das Problem (e)........... problem
das Projekt (e)............. project
das Symbol (e)............ symbol
der Test (s)................. test
der Text (e)................ text
der Titel (-)................. title
die Übersetzung (en) ... translation
die Übung (en)............ exercise
die Vokabel (n)........... vocabulary item
der Wortschatz (-schätze)...... vocabulary list
die Zusammenfassung (en).... summary

das Beispiel (e)............. example
der Fehler (-)................ mistake
die Handschrift .... handwriting
das Kästchen (-) .... box
die Lektüre.................. reading
der Punkt (e) .... full stop; point
die Rechtschreibung .... spelling
der Satz (Sätze)........... sentence
die Seite (n) .... page
die Sprache (n)............ language
das Wort (e) .... word
das Wort (Wörter)........ (individual) word
die Zeile (n) .... line (in text)

die Antwort (en) .... reply, answer
der Dialog (e).............. dialogue
die Disziplin .... discipline
der Erfolg (e) .... success
das Ergebnis (se) .... result
die Erlaubnis (se)........ permission
der Fortschritt (e)........ progress, improvement
die Regel (n) .... rule
die Stille...................... silence
der Unterricht.............. teaching

Die Ausstattung des Klassenzimmers
Classroom equipment

das Bild (er)................ picture
der Bleistift (e)............ pencil
das Buch (Bücher).......book
das Federmäppchen (-) .pencil case
der Filzstift (e)............. felt tip pen
der Füller (-)................ (fountain) pen
das Heft (e) .... exercise book, note book
der Kugelschreiber (-) ..(ball-point) pen
der Kuli (s) .... (ball-point) pen
das Lineal (e) .... ruler
das Notizbuch (-bücher) ... notebook
der Ordner (-) .... folder, file, binder
der Radiergummi (s) ....rubber
das Schmierheft (e).......rough book
der Schreibblock (-blöcke).... notepad
das Schulbuch (-bücher)........ text book
die Schulmappe (n) ......schoolbag
der Stift (e) .... pen
der Taschenrechner (-) .calculator
die Tinte .... ink

der Kleber (-)............... glue stick
der Klebstoff (e) .... glue
die Patrone (n)............. ink cartridge
der Rucksack (-säcke) ..rucksack
die Schultasche (n).......schoolbag
der Spitzer (-) .... pencil sharpener
der Tintenlöscher (-).....eraser pen

das Blatt Papier ....sheet of paper
die Büroklammer (n)....paper clip
der Hefter (-)................ stapler; file
die Heftklammer (n).....staple
die Landkarte (n).........map
der Locher (-) .... hole punch
die Mappe (n)............... briefcase, bag
das Papier .... paper
die Schere (n) .... pair of scissors
der Tesafilm® .... Sellotape®
das Wörterbuch (-bücher). dictionary

Nützliche Verben   **Useful verbs**
ankreuzen † *sep* ....to tick (✓)
aufschreiben *irreg sep* ..to write down
ausradieren † *sep* ....to rub out, erase
ausschneiden *irreg sep*.to cut out
beantworten † ....to answer
durchstreichen *irreg sep*... to cross out
ergänzen † ....to complete
kleben ....to stick, glue
kopieren † ....to copy
korrigieren † ....to correct, mark
ordnen † ....to put in the right order
rechnen † ....to calculate
unterstreichen *irreg insep*..to underline
verbessern † ....to correct
vergleichen *irreg* ....to compare

diskutieren † ....to discuss, chat
erklären † ....to explain
notieren † ....to note
studieren † ....to study
verstehen *irreg*.............to understand
sich vorstellen *sep* ....to imagine

aufpassen † *sep*......to be careful, pay attention
aussprechen *irreg sep* ...to pronounce
bedeuten † ....to mean
enden † ....to end, finish
sich entschuldigen † .....to apologise
übersetzen † *insep* ....to translate
wiederholen *insep*........to repeat

ausfallen* *irreg sep* ......to be cancelled
beaufsichtigen † ....to supervise
erfinden *irreg*...............to invent
erlauben † ....to allow
ermutigen † ....to encourage
Verspätung haben *irreg* .....to be late
herumalbern *sep* ....to play up, mess about
fallen lassen *irreg*........to drop

auswendig lernen ....to learn by heart
ein Experiment machen ...to do an experiment
Hausaufgaben machen . to do one's homework
nachsitzen *irreg sep* ..... to be in detention
plaudern ....to chat
raten *irreg* ....to guess
schwatzen † ....to chat, gossip
anwesend sein* *irreg* ... to be present
eine Frage stellen ....to ask a question
Sport treiben *irreg*....... to play sport
unterrichten *insep*........to teach
wählen ....to choose

Wie ist es?   **What is it like?**
abwesend.....................absent, away
anwesend.....................present, here
fleißig ....hard-working
Lieblings- ....favourite
streng...........................strict
gesprächig ....talkative
gewissenhaft................conscientious
Schul- ....to do with school

dumm ....stupid
durchschnittlich............average
einfach..........................easy
falsch............................wrong
genau ....exact, precise
kompliziert ....complicated
nützlich........................useful
nutzlos..........................useless
richtig ....right, true
schrecklich ....awful
schwierig.....................difficult

schwach in...................weak, not good (at)
stark in..........................good (at)
nicht gut in ....not good at

25

Die Prüfungen   Exams

die Note (n)................. mark
das Zeugnis (se) .... report

1	sehr gut	very good
2	gut	good
3	befriedigend	satisfactory
4	ausreichend	adequate
5	mangelhaft	weak
6	ungenügend...........	unsatisfactory

das Abitur..................... A level
der Hauptschulabschluss (-schlüsse)
            .... GCSE/GNVQ
der Realschulabschluss (-schlüsse)
            .... GCSE/GNVQ
die Klausur (en)........... end of module test
der Kurs (e).................. course
die Prüfung (en)........... exam
die mündliche Prüfung ......speaking test
die schriftliche Prüfung .....writing exam

For **choice of study** see page 71

die Antwort (en) .... answer
die falsche Antwort ..... wrong answer
die richtige Antwort..... right answer
die Arbeit.................... work
das Ergebnis (se).......... result
das Examen (-)............. degree exam
die Frage (n) .... question
die Klassenarbeit (en).. assessment/class test

das Niveau (s) .... level
das Resultat (e) .... result
der Unterricht .... teaching

Nützliche Verben   **Useful verbs**

abschreiben *irreg sep* ...to copy
bestehen *irreg*............... to pass (exam)
sitzen bleiben* *irreg*..... to repeat a class
durchfallen* *irreg sep* ..to fail (exam)
Recht haben *irreg*......... to be right
Unrecht haben *irreg* ..... to be wrong
mogeln........................... to cheat
studieren † .... to study
versetzt werden* *irreg* .to move up a class
wiederholen *insep* .... to revise

AGs   Out of school activities

die AG (s).................... school club
der Ausflug (-flüge)...... trip, outing
der Austausch (e)......... exchange
der Besuch (e)............. visit
die Blaskapelle (n) .... brass band
der Chor (Chöre) .... choir
der Klub (s) .... club
die Mannschaft (en) ..... team
das Orchester (-) .... orchestra
das Spiel (e)................. match
das Theaterstück (e)...... play
das Tournier (e) .... tournament
der Verein (e) .... club

Phrases

Was wirst du nächstes Jahr machen? *What are you going to do next year?*

Ich werde die Schule verlassen *I'm going to leave school*

Ich werde mit meinem Vater arbeiten *I'm going to work with my father*

Ich werde eine Lehre als Elektriker machen *I am going to do an apprenticeship as an electrician*

Ich gehe in die Oberstufe *I'm going into the Sixth Form/Year 12*

Ich werde Biologie, Erdkunde, Mathe und Deutsch lernen
    I'm going to do biology, geography, maths and German

HOLIDAY TIME AND TRAVEL

2A   TRAVEL, TRANSPORT, FINDING THE WAY

Wie komme ich am besten …? How do I get to …?

Entschuldigen Sie, bitte! ...Excuse me
Gehen Sie geradeaus! ...Go straight on
Nehmen Sie die B52! ...Take the B52
Biegen Sie rechts ab! ....Turn right
Biegen Sie links ab!......Turn left
Gehen Sie über die Straße!. Cross the road
Vielen Dank! ....Thank you very much

For **buildings** see page 17
For **landmarks** see page 18

Wo ist das?   Where is it?

10 Kilometer von .... 10 km from
an der Ampel vorbei..... past the crossroads
an der Straßenecke .... on the street corner
vor dem Kiosk............. in front of the kiosk
neben der Post .... next to the post office
hinter dem Theater .... behind the theatre
vor dem Kino .... outside the cinema
gegenüber der Bank ..... opposite the bank
in der Nähe vom Platz.. near the square
ganz in der Nähe .... close by
hier in der Nähe........... near here

Phrases

Wie komme ich am besten zum Bahnhof, bitte? *How do I get to the station, please?*

Gehen Sie die Straße entlang! Dann nehmen Sie die erste Straße rechts!
  Go along the street. Then take the first on the right

Nehmen Sie die zweite Straße links *Take the second on the left*

Ist es weit? *Is it far?* Wie weit ist es? *How far is it?*

Das ist ganz in der Nähe. Es ist fünf Minuten zu Fuß, nicht weit vom Rathaus entfernt
  It's very near. It's a five minute walk, not far from the town hall

Schilder   Signs

Anlieger frei ....residents only
Ausstieg......................get off here
Baustelle ....road works
bitte einordnen.............get in lane
den Rasen nicht betreten ..keep off the grass
Deutsche Bahn (DB) ....German railways
Einbahnstraße ....one way street
Einstieg......................get on here
Fußgängerzone ....pedestrian zone
Halteverbot..................no stopping
keine Zufahrt ....no entry
Parkverbot ....no parking
Rad fahren verboten .....no cycling

Straße gesperrt ....road closed
Umleitung ....diversion
zu den Gleisen.............to the platforms

For **shop signs** see page 63

Verkehrsmittel   Means of transport

das Auto (s) .... car
der Bus (se) .... bus
der Dampfer (-) .... steamer, riverboat
das Fahrrad (-räder) ...... bike
das Flugzeug (e) .... plane
der Hubschrauber (-) .... helicopter
der Lastwagen (-) .... lorry

der Lieferwagen (-) ...... van
der LKW (s) .... lorry
das Mofa (s) .... moped
das Motorrad (-räder) ... motorbike
das Mountainbike (s) ... mountain bike
der PKW (s) .... car
der Reisebus (se) .... coach
der Roller (-) .... scooter
die S-Bahn (en) .... city railway
die Straßenbahn (en).... tram
das Taxi (s) .... taxi
die U-Bahn (en) .... underground, metro
die öffentlichen Verkehrsmittel *pl*
 .... public transport
der Wagen (-).............. car
der Zug (Züge) .... train

Bahnreisen   Train travel

die Abfahrt (en) .... departure
die Abreise (n) .... departure
die Ankunft .... arrival
die Auskunft .... information
die Bahn..................... railway
die Eisenbahn .... railway
der Fahrplan (-pläne) ... timetable
die Reise (n)................ journey
die Verbindung (en)..... connection
die Verspätung (en) ..... delay
das Ziel (e) .... destination
der Zuschlag (Zuschläge)..supplement

der D-Zug (-züge) .... express train
der Eilzug (-züge) .... regional express train
der ICE-Zug (-Züge).... Inter-City train
der Inter-Regio............ regional express
der Nahverkehrszug..... local train
der Nichtraucher .... non-smoker
der Personenzug (-züge) ...slow train
der Schnellzug (-züge). express train
der Zug (Züge) .... train

die einfache Fahrkarte (n) .single ticket
die Fahrkarte (n).......... ticket
der Fahrschein (e)........ ticket
die Rückfahrkarte (n) ... return ticket
die Reservierung (en)... reservation

erster Klasse .... first class
zweiter Klasse .... second class

der Bahnhof (-höfe) ...... railway station
die Bahnhofshalle (n) ... station foyer
der Bahnsteig (e) .... platform
DB (Deutsche Bahn) .... German railways
der Fahrkartenschalter (-) ... ticket office
das Gepäck .... luggage
die Gepäckaufbewahrung .. left luggage
das Gepäckschließfach (-fächer)
 .... left luggage locker
das Gleis (e)................. platform, track number
der Hauptbahnhof........ main station
der Taxistand.............. taxi rank
der Wartesaal (-säle)..... waiting room

das Abteil (e) .... compartment
der Liegewagen (-) .... couchette car
der Schlafwagen (-)...... sleeping car
der Speisewagen (-)...... dining/buffet car
der Wagen (-) .... carriage

besetzt......................... occupied
frei .... free
planmäßig................... according to timetable
pünktlich..................... on time
verspätet .... late
werktags .... on Monday to Saturday
wochentags.................. on weekdays

abfahren* *irreg sep* ...... to leave (from)
abholen *sep*................. to meet, pick up
ankommen* *irreg sep*... to arrive
aussteigen* *irreg sep*.... to get off/out of
einsteigen* *irreg sep* .... to get on/into

erreichen † ....to reach

mit dem Zug fahren* *irreg* .... to go by train

kontrollieren † ....to examine, check

den Zug nehmen *irreg*.. to catch the train

umsteigen* *irreg sep*.... to change trains

verpassen †.................. to miss (train, etc)

Phrases

Wann fährt der nächste Zug nach Berlin, bitte? *When does the next train to Berlin leave?*

Der Zug fährt um neun Uhr ab *The train leaves at 9.00*

Zweimal einfach nach München *Two singles to Munich*

Einmal hin und zurück nach Hannover *One return ticket to Hanover*

Der Zug hat zwanzig Minuten Verspätung *The train is 20 minutes late*

Die Fahrkarte kostet hundert Euro *The ticket costs 100 euros*

Es gibt einen Zuschlag von fünfundzwanzig Euro für den ICE-Zug
There is a 25 euro supplement for the high speed ICE train

Bus und Straßenbahn
Bus and tram travel

der Busbahnhof (-höfe).bus station

die Bushaltestelle (n)....bus stop

der Lautsprecher (-) ......loudspeaker

die Linie (n)..................line, route

die Nummer (n)............number

der Entwerter (-) ....ticket validating machine

die Fahrkarte (n)...........ticket

der Fahrkartenautomat (en) *wk*
..............................ticket machine

der Fahrpreis (e)........... fare

die Kontrolle (n) .... check (of tickets)

die Streifenkarte (n) ..... book of tickets

die Zehnerkarte (n)....... book of ten tickets

entwerten † .... to time stamp a ticket

mit dem Bus fahren* *irreg*.....to go by bus

mit dem Reisebus fahren*......to go by coach

Phrases

Ein Bus fährt alle zehn Minuten *There is a bus every 10 minutes*

Der Bus hat eine Panne *The bus has broken down*

Die Überfahrt   Crossing the Channel

die Fähre (n) ....car ferry

der Fährhafen (-häfen)..ferry terminal

der Hafen (Häfen).........port

der Kanaltunnel ....Channel Tunnel

das Meer (e)..................sea

das Schiff (e)................ship

die Überfahrt (en).........crossing

glatt..............................smooth

seekrank........................seasick

stürmisch .... rough (crossing)

an Bord........................ on board

auf Deck gehen* *irreg* .to go up on deck

Das Flugreisen   Flying

der Flughafen (-häfen).. airport

das Flugzeug (e) .... plane

der Jumbojet (s)............ jumbo jet

die Maschine (n) .... plane

die Kabine (n) .... cabin

die Ansage (n) .... call
der Flug (Flüge) .... flight
der Flugsteig (e) .... gate
die Landung (en) .... landing
der Passagier (e) .... passenger
die Pünktlichkeit .... punctuality
der Sicherheitsgurt (e) . seat belt
die Touristenklasse ...... tourist class
die Verspätung (en) ..... delay

abfliegen* *irreg sep* ..... to depart (plane)
bestätigen † .... to confirm
einchecken *sep* .... to check in
fliegen* *irreg* .... to fly (person)
kontrollieren † .... to examine, check
landen* † .... to land
starten* † .... to take off (plane)

Mit dem Auto fahren   Going by car

die Ampel .... traffic lights
die Autobahn (en) .... motorway
die Baustelle (n) .... roadworks
der Bürgersteig (e) .... pavement
die Kreuzung (en) .... crossroads
das Parkhaus (-häuser) . multi-storey car park
der Parkplatz (-plätze) . car park
die Tankstelle (n) .... petrol station
die Tiefgarage (n) .... underground car park
die Toilette (n) .... toilet

die Ausfahrt .... motorway exit
das Autobahnnetz .... motorway network
die Bundesstraße (en) .. main road
die Kurve (n) .... bend

die Landstraße (n) .... secondary road
der Rastplatz (-plätze) .. picnic area
der Rasthof (-höfe) ...... service area
die Raststätte (n) .... service area
der Stau (s) .... traffic jam, delay
das Straßenschild (er) ... road sign
der Verkehrskreisel ...... roundabout

das Ende (n) .... end
die Fahrschule (n) .... driving school
der Führerschein (e) ..... driving licence
die Gefahr (en) .... danger
die Geschwindigkeit (en) ...... speed
die Hauptverkehrszeit (en) .... rush hour
die Landkarte (n) .... map
die Straßenverkehrsordnung . highway code
die Umleitung (en) .... diversion
die Vorfahrt .... right of way, priority
die Werkstatt (-stätten) ...... garage (repairs)

abbiegen* *irreg sep* ...... to turn (off road)
den Motor anlassen *irreg sep*
   .... to start the engine
die Scheinwerfer anmachen *sep*
   .... to switch on headlights
die Reifen nachsehen *irreg sep*
   .... to check the tyres
bremsen .... to brake
fahren* *irreg* (+ sein) ... to travel, go
fahren *irreg* (+ haben) .. to drive (a vehicle)
rückwärts fahren* *irreg* ..... to reverse
eine Panne haben *irreg* ...... to break down
parken .... to park
überqueren *insep* .... to cross
voll tanken .... to fill up with fuel

Phrases

Verkaufen Sie Stadtpläne, bitte? *Do you sell town plans, please?*

Wo ist die Sparkasse bitte? *Where is the bank, please?*

Schauen Sie sich den Plan an. Sie ist neben dem Dom. *Look at the plan. It's near the cathedral*

Sie ist in einem großen Gebäude aus Backstein/Sandstein *It's in a large brick/sandstone building*

2B   TOURISM

Tourismus	Tourism
der Aufenthalt (e)	stay
das Ausland	abroad
die Fahrt (en)	journey
die Ferien *pl*	holidays
die Gegend (en)	region
das Informationsbüro (s)	tourist office

das Land (Länder)	country
die Reise (n)	journey
das Reisebüro	travel agency
der Reisepass (-pässe)	passport
der Stadtplan (-pläne)	town plan
das Verkehrsamt (-ämter)	tourist office
die Wechselstube (n)	bureau de change

Phrases

Was gibt es in der Gegend zu sehen und zu tun? *What is there to see and do in the area?*

Haben sie einen Prospekt und ein Hotelverzeichnis? *Do you have a brochure and a list of hotels?*

Die Ausflüge	Outings
der Ausflug (-flüge)	trip, outing
der Freizeitpark (s)	amusement park
die Klassenfahrt (en)	school trip
die Kirmes	funfair
das Picknick (s)	picnic
die Rundfahrt (en)	guided tour (coach, etc)
der Safaripark (s)	safari park
die Sehenswürdigkeiten *pl*	sights
der Spaziergang (-gänge)	walk
der Stadtbummel	stroll around town
die Tour (en)	tour
die Wanderung (en)	long walk

Leute	People
der Besitzer (-)	owner
der Busfahrer (-)	coach driver
der Camper (-)	camper
die Empfangsdame (n)	receptionist
die Herbergseltern *pl*	youth hostel wardens (couple)
die Herbergsmutter	youth hostel warden
der Herbergsvater	youth hostel warden
der Kellner (-)	waiter
die Kellnerin (nen)	waitress
der Reiseleiter (-)	group leader, courier
der Reisende ‡	traveller

der Tourist (en) *wk*	tourist
die Touristin (nen)	tourist
der Urlauber (-)	holiday maker

Die Unterkunft	Lodging
der Campingplatz (-plätze)	camp site
die Ferienwohnung (en)	holiday home
das Hotel (s)	hotel
die Jugendherberge (n)	youth hostel
die Pension (en)	boarding house

Fremdenzimmer	room available
Luxus-	luxury
Halbpension	half board
Vollpension	full board
Zimmer frei	room available

bequem	comfortable
besetzt	taken, occupied
frei	available
(nicht) gestattet	(not) allowed
inbegriffen	included
luxuriös	luxurious
privat	private
voll	full
übernachten † *insep*	to stay the night

31

Wie viele Personen? For how many?
der Erwachsene (n) ‡ ... adult
der Junge (n) *wk* .... boy
das Kind (er) .... child
das Mädchen (-) .... girl
die Person (en) .... person
bis drei Jahre .... under three years old

Wann bist du gefahren?
                    When did you go?
am Wochenende .... at the weekend
im Sommer .... in summer
im Winter .... in winter
in den Sommerferien ... in the summer holidays
letzte Woche .... last week
vor zwei Monaten .... two months ago
vor zwei Wochen .... a fortnight ago
letztes Jahr .... last year

Wann fährst du?   When are you going?
zu Weihnachten .... at Christmas
zu Ostern .... at Easter
im August .... in August
morgen .... tomorrow
übermorgen .... the day after tomorrow
nächste Woche .... next week
in einer Woche .... in a week's time
in drei Monaten .... in three months' time
nächstes Jahr .... next year
in der Zukunft .... in the future

Mit wem?   With whom?
mit meiner Familie ...... with my family
mit meinem Freund ...... with my friend (male)
mit meiner Freundin .... with my friend (female)
mit meinen Freunden ... with my friends

Für wie lange?   For how long?
für einen Tag .... for a day
für einen Monat .... for a month
für eine Nacht .... for a night
für eine Woche .... for a week
für drei Tage .... for three days

für vier Nächte .... for four nights
für zwei Wochen .... for a fortnight

Wohin?   Where to?
ins Ausland .... abroad
in die Berge .... to the mountains
auf das Land .... to the country
zum See .... to the lake
zum Strand .... to the beach
in den Wald .... to the forest

beliebt .... popular
bildschön .... picturesque
einmalig .... unforgettable
friedlich .... peaceful
historisch .... historic
hübsch .... pretty
sehenswert .... worth seeing

auf Urlaub sein* *irreg* ...... to be on holiday
in Urlaub fahren* *irreg* ..... to go on holiday
besichtigen † .... to visit (tourist attraction)
packen .... to pack
spazieren gehen* *irreg* ...... to go for walk
wandern* .... to go for a hike

Ich brauche ...   I need ...
einen Ausweis .... an identity card
einen Fotoapparat .... a camera
einen Koffer .... a case
einen Pass .... a passport
einen Rucksack .... a rucksack
einen Stadtplan .... a town plan
eine Broschüre .... a brochure
eine Landkarte .... a map
eine Mitgliedskarte ...... a membership card
eine Sonnenbrille .... sunglasses
ein Foto .... a photo

Ich kaufte ...   I bought ...
ein Andenken .... a souvenir
Ansichtskarten .... postcards

Aufkleber......................stickers
Kekse...........................biscuits
Pralinen........................chocolates
eine Puppe....................a doll
einen Schlüsselring.......a key ring
Souvenirs......................souvenirs
Süßwaren......................sweets
ein T-Shirt....................a T-shirt

Einen Austausch mitmachen
Going on an exchange

der Brieffreund (e)........penfriend
die Brieffreundin (nen).penfriend
die deutsche Familie.....German family
die englische Familie....English family
der Lehrer (-)................teacher
die Lehrerin (nen)........teacher

der Ausflug (-flüge)......trip, outing
die Dauer......................length (stay, lesson)
die Freizeit...................free time
die Gastfreundschaft.....hospitality
das Heimweh................home-sickness
die deutsche Küche......German cooking
die englische Küche.....English cooking
das Lernprogramm (e)..curriculum
die Reise (n).................journey
die Schule (n)...............school
die Schuluniform..........school uniform
der Sport......................sport
die Städtepartnerschaft .town twinning
die Stunden...................lessons
das Taschengeld...........pocket money

auspacken *sep*...............to unpack
besuchen †....................to visit
organisieren †...............to arrange, organise
vergleichen *irreg* mit (+ Dat)
................................to compare with

For **opinions** see page 78

Das Wetter   Weather

das Satellitenbild (er)...satellite picture
die Vorhersage (n).......forecast
die Wetterlage (n)........weather conditions
die Wettervorhersage (n)..weather forecast
der Wetterbericht (e)....weather report

das Gewitter (-).............thunderstorm
die Höchsttemperatur (en)...highest temperature
der Nebel (-).................fog
der Regen....................rain
der Schauer (-)..............shower
der Schnee...................snow
die Sonne (n)................sun
der Sturm (Stürme)......storm
die Temperatur (en).....temperature
die Tiefsttemperatur (en)....lowest temperature
der Wind (e)................wind
die Wolke (n)..............cloud

die Aufheiterung (en)...bright period
der Donner...................thunder
das Eis.........................ice
die Feuchtigkeit...........humidity
der Grad.......................degree
der Himmel..................sky
die Hitze......................heat
das Klima (s)...............climate
das Meer (e).................sea
der Mond (e)................moon
der Niederschlag..........precipitation
................................(rain or snow)
der Schatten.................shadow, shade
der Sonnenschein.........sunshine

der Blitz (e).................flash of lightning
der Druck....................pressure
der Dunst.....................mist, haze
der Hagel.....................hail
der Hochdruck..............high pressure
der Regenbogen (-bögen)..rainbow
die Sichtweite..............visibility

das Thermometer (-) .... thermometer
der Tiefdruck .... low pressure
die Verbesserung (en).. improvement

Wie ist das Wetter?
What is the weather like?

Es ist 30 Grad .... It is 30 degrees
Es ist dunkel .... It is dark
Es ist heiß .... It is hot
Es ist hell .... It is light
Es ist kalt .... It is cold
Es ist neblig .... It is foggy
Es ist niederschlagsfrei It is dry
Es ist schön .... It is fine
Es ist sonnig................. It is sunny
Es ist stürmisch........... It is stormy
Es ist windig .... It is windy
Es ist wolkig .... It is cloudy
Das Wetter ist schlecht ......The weather is bad

Es blitzt........................ It is lightning
Es donnert.................... It is thundering
Es friert .... It is freezing
Es hagelt .... It is hailing
Es regnet .... It is raining
Es schneit.................... It is snowing

Es gibt Frost................ There is frost
Es gibt Gewitter .... There are thunderstorms
Es gibt Nebel .... There is fog
Es gibt Schnee .... There is snow

Wann?   ## When?

ab und zu .... from time to time
gewöhnlich .... usually
manchmal .... sometimes
morgen........................ tomorrow
neulich .... recently
oft .... often
übermorgen................. the day after tomorrow

Adjektive   **Adjectives**
bedeckt ....very cloudy
besser...........................better
bewölkt........................cloudy
blau..............................blue
diesig .:.........................misty, hazy
heftig ....heavy (rain, etc)
heiß..............................hot
heiter............................sunny, bright
herrlich ....gorgeous
mäßig...........................moderate
mild ....mild
nass..............................wet
regnerisch ....rainy
schwül ....heavy, sultry
sonnig...........................sunny
stürmisch ....stormy
trocken.........................dry
trüb ....dull
veränderlich..................variable
wolkenlos ....cloudless
wolkig..........................cloudy

bersten* *irreg* ....to burst
donnern........................to thunder
frieren* *irreg*...............to freeze
regnen † ....to rain
scheinen *irreg*..............to shine
schneien.......................to snow
verändern † ....to change
vorhersagen *sep*...........to forecast
wehen ....to blow (wind)
kälter werden* *irreg*.....to get colder

For **holidays** see page 37
For **celebrations** see pages 50, 68
For **restaurants** see page 39
For **opinions** see page 78

2C ACCOMMODATION

Das Hotel   The hotel

das Doppelzimmer (-)...double room
das Einzelzimmer (-) ....single room
das Familienzimmer (-) family room
das Formular (e)............form
der Preis (e) ....price
die Übernachtung (en)..overnight stay
das Zimmer (-)..............room

die Anmeldung.............reception
der Ausgang (-gänge) ...exit
das Badezimmer (-) ......bathroom
der Eingang (-gänge) ....entrance
der Empfang (-fänge) ...reception
das Erdgeschoss...........ground floor
der Fahrstuhl (-stühle)..lift
der Keller (-)................basement
der Notausgang (-gänge) ..emergency exit
der Parkplatz (-plätze)..car park
das Restaurant (s).........restaurant
der Stock (Stöcke).......storey
die Toiletten *pl*............toilets
die Treppe (n)..............stairs

Das Schlafzimmer   Bedroom

das Bad........................bath
das Bett (en)................bed
die Bettdecke (n).........blanket
das Betttuch (-tücher)...sheet
das Bettzeug *no pl*.......bedding
das Doppelbett (en)......double bed
die Dusche (n).............shower
der Fernseher (-)..........TV set
das Handtuch (-tücher).towel
der Kleiderbügel (-)......coathanger
der Kleiderschrank (-schränke).....wardrobe
das Kopfkissen (-) ....pillow
das Laken (-)................sheet
der Schlüssel (-) ....key
die Seife ....soap
die Steppdecke (n) ....duvet, quilt
das Telefon (e).............telephone
die Wolldecke (n) ....blanket

die Empfangsdame (n).receptionist
der Geschäftsführer (-).manager
der Inhaber (-) ....owner
das Zimmermädchen (-) ....chambermaid

Phrases

Gibt es einen Parkplatz? *Is there a car park?*

Ja, man kann hinter dem Hotel parken *Yes, you can park behind the hotel*

Wo sind die Toiletten? *Where are the toilets?*

Im Keller *In the basement*

Das Restaurant ist im Erdgeschoss *The restaurant is on the ground floor*

Man darf im Restaurant nicht rauchen *Smoking is not allowed in the restaurant*

Was kostet eine Übernachtung? *How much is it per night?*

Man kann zwischen sieben Uhr und zehn Uhr frühstücken
    You can have breakfast between 7 and 10

Das Abendessen wird ab sechs Uhr serviert *Evening meal is served from 6 o'clock*

Im Zimmer 15 fehlen Handtücher *There are no towels in room 15*

Es ist zu laut - wir möchten ein anderes Zimmer haben
    It's too noisy - we'd like to change rooms

Der Campingplatz The campsite

das Camping .... camping
das Camping Carnet (s)......camping carnet
der Empfang .... reception
das Freibad (-bäder) ..... open air pool
die Sanitäranlage (n) ... toilet block
der Stellplatz (-plätze) . pitch
der Waschraum (-räume)...washroom
der Wohnwagen (-)...... caravan
das Zelt (e) .... tent
der Zuschlag (Zuschläge)...supplement

der elektrische Anschluss ..electric hook-up
das Spülbecken (-) ....washing up sink
warmes Essen zum Mitnehmen
...........................cooked take-away meals
die Wäscherei .... laundry

die Campingausrüstung .....camping equipment
der Campingkocher (-)......camping stove
die Lebensmittel *pl* ...... food(stuff)s
der Schlafsack (-säcke) sleeping bag
die Streichhölzer *pl* ...... matches
die Taschenlampe (n) .. torch
das Taschenmesser (-).. pocket knife

der Radverleih............. cycle hire
(Kein) Trinkwasser...... (non) drinking water
die Wäsche .... washing (clothes)
die Waschmaschine (n) .....washing machine

im Schatten .... shady
in der Sonne............... sunny
im Freien..................... in the open air

ein Zelt abbauen *sep*.....to take down tent
ein Zelt aufschlagen *irreg sep*.to put up tent
campen ....to camp
grillen ....to barbecue, grill
zelten † ....to camp

Die Jugendherberge   Youth hostel

das Büro (s) ....office
DJH ....German youth hostel
die Küche (n)...............kitchen
der Schlafraum (-räume) .. dormitory
der Speisesaal (-säle)....dining room
der Tagesraum (-räume)... day room

der Abfalleimer (-) ....rubbish bin
die Bettwäsche ....linen
die Decke (n)...............blanket
der Leinenschlafsack (-säcke)
................................sheet sleeping bag
heißes Wasser........hot water
kaltes Wasser.........cold water

bezahlen † ....to pay
buchen ....to book
mieten † ....to hire
reservieren † ....to reserve, book
unterschreiben *irreg insep*.. to sign

For **food** see page 52
For **restaurant** see page 39
For **weather** see page 33
For **holiday activities** see page 37
For **days, months, seasons** see page 86, 87

2D HOLIDAY ACTIVITIES

Am Meer   At the seaside

das Kino (s)..................cinema
der Nachtklub (s)..........night club
das Schwimmbad (bäder) . swimming pool

das (Ruder)boot (e)......(rowing) boat
das Schlauchboot (e).....inflatable dinghy
das Segelboot (e) ....dinghy
das Surfbrett (er)..........sailboard

For **outings** see page 31

der Badeort (e).............seaside resort
die Ebbe......................low tide
das Eis.........................ice cream
der Eisverkäufer (-)......ice cream seller
der Fischer (-) ....fisherman
die Flut ....high tide
der Hafen (Häfen).........port
der Kai (s)...................quay
die Küste (n)................coast
der Leuchtturm (-türme) ... lighthouse
die Möwe (n)...............seagull
die Muschel (n) ....shell
der Rettungsring (e)......lifebelt

der Sand ....sand
die Sandburg (en)........sandcastle
die See (n)...................sea
der Strand (Strände) ..... beach
der (un)überwachte Strand
.... (un)supervised beach
der Strandkorb (-körbe)..... wicker wind-break
die Welle (n) .... wave (sea)

die Angelrute (n).........fishing rod
der Eimer (-)................bucket
die Sonnenbrille (n) ..... sunglasses
der Sonnenhut (-hüte) .. sunhat
das Sonnenöl ....sun oil
der Spaten (-)...............spade

baden †........................to bathe
rudern ....to row
schwimmen (*) *irreg* ... to swim, bathe
segeln ....to sail
sich sonnen...................to sunbathe
spazieren gehen* *irreg*.to go for a walk
surfen ....to surf
tauchen*......................to dive
windsurfen ....to windsurf

Phrases

Ich windsurfe gern *I like sailboarding*
Mein Bruder segelt lieber *My brother prefers sailing*

Wintersport   Winter sports

Der Wintersportort   Ski resort
der Berg (e)..................mountain
die Eisbahn (en)............ice rink
der Gletscher (-)...........glacier
der Hang (Hänge) ....slope
die Hütte (n) ....mountain refuge

die Lawine (n)..............avalanche
die Piste (n).................piste, ski run
der Schnee...................snow
die Seilbahn (en) ....cable car
die Sesselbahn (en) ......chair lift
das Snowboarden ....snowboarding

Leute	People
der Anfänger (-)	beginner
der Skiführer (-)	guide
der Skilehrer (-)	ski instructor
der Skifahrer (-)	skier

Skiausrüstung	Skiing equipment
der Handschuh (e)	glove
die Mütze (n)	hat
die Skibrille (n)...........	ski goggles
die Skier *pl*	skis
die Skihose (n)............	salopettes
die Skistiefel *pl*...........	ski boots
der Skistock (-stöcke) ..	ski pole

Schlitten fahren* *irreg.* to go sledging
Ski laufen* *sep irreg* ... to ski
Snowboard fahren**irreg*...to go snowboarding
Winterurlaub machen .. to take a winter holiday

For **opinions** see page 78
For **outings** see page 31

Essen und Trinken
Eating and drinking

Schilder	Signs
durchgehende warme Küche .hot food all day	
Erfrischungen	refreshments
Tagesmenü...................	day's set price menu
Tagesgericht................	dish of the day
zum Mitnehmen...........	take-away

Ausrufe	Exclamations
Fräulein!	Waitress!
Herr Ober!	Waiter!
Guten Appetit!	Enjoy your meal!
Mahlzeit!	Enjoy your meal!
Prost!	Cheers!
Zum Wohl!	Cheers!
Ich bin satt	I've eaten enough

(nein) danke................. (no) thank you
Zahlen bitte! .... The bill, please

Die Mahlzeiten	Meals
das Abendbrot (e)	evening meal (cold)
das Abendessen (-)	dinner, evening meal
das Frühstück (e)	breakfast
der Imbiss (-e)	snack
Kaffee und Kuchen	afternoon coffee
das Mittagessen (-)	lunch, midday meal

Wo kann man essen?	Where can you eat?
die Bar (s)....................	bar
das Café (s)..................	café
das Gasthaus (-häuser)..	pub, inn
der Gasthof (-höfe).......	pub, inn
die Gaststätte (n)	pub
die Imbisshalle (n)........	snack bar
die Imbissstube (n).......	snack bar
die Kneipe (n)	pub
die Konditorei (en).......	café; cake shop
der Ratskeller (-)	town hall cellar restaurant
das Restaurant (s)	restaurant
der Schnellimbiss (-e) ..snack bar
das Stehcafé (s)............	quick café
die Weinstube (n).........	wine bar
die Wirtschaft (en)	pub
das Wirtshaus (-häuser) hotel
die Wurstbude (n)	sausage stand

Leute	People
der Gast (Gäste)...........	guest
der Inhaber (-)..............	owner
der Kassierer (-)...........	till operator
der Kellner (-)..............	waiter
die Kellnerin (nen)	waitress
der Koch (Köche).........	cook, chef
die Köchin (nen)	cook, chef
der Kunde (n) *wk*.........	customer
die Kundin (nen)	customer

Im Restaurant   In a restaurant

am Fenster ....by the window
auf der Terrasse ....on the terrace
draußen ....outside
drinnen.........................inside

die Toiletten *pl* ....toilets
die Auswahl.................choice
die britische Küche.......British food
die deutsche Küche .....German food
die italienische Küche ..Italian food
die Spezialität (en).......speciality

der Geruch (Gerüche)...smell
der Geschmack (Geschmäcke)
................................taste, flavour
die Portion (en)............portion

die Bedienung...............service, service charge
das Kuvert (s)...............cover charge
die MwSt ....VAT
die Quittung (en) ....receipt
die Rechnung (en) ....bill
das Trinkgeld (er) ....tip (money)
der Zettel (-).................chit
(nicht) inbegriffen.........(not) included
inbegr/einschl/inkl ....included

Die Speisekarte   Menu

die Vorspeise (n) ....starter
das Gericht (e) ....dish
das Hauptgericht (e)......main course
die Tageskarte (n)........menu of the day
der Nachtisch (e) ....dessert
die Weinkarte (n).........wine list

Die Vorspeisen   Starters

der Aufschnitt ....mixed cold meats
die Hühnerbrühe...........chicken soup
die Leberwurst..............liver sausage
die Pastete (n)..............pâté
die kalte Platte ....mixed cold meats

die Suppe (n)...............soup
der Tomatensalat (e).....tomato salad
die Wurst (Würste) ......salami, sausage

Das Hauptgericht   Main course

der Braten....................roast meat
das Brathähnchen (-) ....roast chicken
der Eintopf (Eintöpfe)..casserole, stew
das Kalbschnitzel (-) ....veal escalope
das Kotelett (s) ....chop, cutlet
das Omelett (s) ....omelette
die Pizza (s).................pizza
der Rinderbraten...........roast beef
der Sauerbraten ....pickled roast beef
das Schweinekotelett (s)... pork chop
das Schweineschnitzel (-). pork escalope
das Steak (s) ....steak

Gemüse   Vegetables

die Bohnen *pl* ....beans
die Erbsen *pl* ....peas
die Kartoffeln *pl*..........potatoes
die Pommes (Frites).....chips
der Reis ....rice
der Salat ....salad
die Salzkartoffeln *pl*.....boiled potatoes

Der Nachtisch   Dessert

der Apfelkuchen (-)......apple tart
der Apfelstrudel (-).......apple strudel
der Eisbecher...............ice cream sundae
der Joghurt (s) ....yoghurt
der Käsekuchen (-).......cheesecake
das Kompott ....stewed fruit
der Kuchen (-).............gâteau
der Obstsalat................fruit salad
der Pudding (-) ....cold milk dessert
die Schlagsahne...........whipped cream
das Schokoladeneis ......chocolate ice cream
die Torte (n) ....gateau, flan
das Vanilleeis ....vanilla ice cream

Auf dem Tisch	**On the table**
der Becher (-)	mug
das Besteck	cutlery
die Flasche (n)	bottle
die Gabel (n)	fork
das Geschirr	crockery
das Glas (Gläser)	glass
die Kaffeekanne (n)	coffee pot
der Kaffeelöffel (n)	teaspoon
der Korkenzieher (-)	corkscrew
der Krug (Krüge)	jug
der Löffel (-)	spoon
das Messer (-)	knife
der Pfeffer	pepper (spice)
das Salz	salt
die Schale (n)	bowl
der Senf	mustard
die Serviette (n)	serviette, napkin
die Tasse (n)	cup
die Teekanne (n)	teapot
der Teller (-)	plate
die Tischdecke (n)	tablecloth
die Untertasse (n)	saucer

Im Café — At the café

Getränke	**Drinks**
der Apfelsaft	apple juice
das Bier	beer
die Cola	cola
der Kaffee	coffee
der Kakao	cocoa
das Kännchen (-)	individual pot
die Limo (s)	lemonade
die Limonade (n)	lemonade
das Mineralwasser	mineral water
der Orangensaft (-säfte)	orange juice
das Pils	lager
der Rotwein (e)	red wine
der Saft (Säfte)	fruit juice
der Schnaps	spirits
die Schokolade	chocolate
der Sprudel	fizzy water; lemonade

der Tee	tea
der Wein (e)	wine
der Weißwein (e)	white wine
der Zitronentee	lemon tea

Der Imbiß	**A snack**
ein belegtes Brot	open sandwich
der Berliner	doughnut
die Bockwurst (-würste)	frankfurter
die Bratwurst (-würste)	fried sausage
das Butterbrot (e)	sandwich
die Chips *pl*	crisps
die Currywurst (-würste)	curried sausage
das Ei (er)	egg
ein hart gekochtes Ei	hard boiled egg
das Eis	ice cream
die Frikadelle (n)	rissole
die Fritten *pl*	chips
das Gebäck *no pl*	biscuits
der Hamburger (-)	beefburger
die Jägerwurst (-würste)	sausage with mushroom sauce
das Käsebrot (e)	cheese sandwich
der Kaugummi	chewing gum
der Ketchup	tomato ketchup
die Mayonnaise	mayonnaise
die Pommes (Frites) *pl*	chips
das Rührei	scrambled egg
das Schinkenbrot (e)	ham sandwich
der Senf	mustard
das Spiegelei	fried egg
der Toast (s)	toast
die Waffel (n)	waffle (edible)
das Würstchen (-)	small sausage
die Zigeunerwurst (-würste)	sausage with paprika sauce

Nützliche Verben	**Useful verbs**
bestellen †	to order
zu Abend essen *irreg*	to have evening meal
zu Mittag essen *irreg*	to have lunch
frühstücken	to have breakfast
Durst haben *irreg*	to be thirsty

Hunger haben *irreg* ......to be hungry
kosten † ....to cost
lieben ....to love
probieren †.....................to try
reservieren † ....to reserve
riechen *irreg* ....to smell
schmecken ....to taste
wählen ....to choose
durstig werden* *irreg* ...to get thirsty
hungrig werden* *irreg*..to get hungry

anbieten *irreg sep*.........to offer
bedienen † ....to serve
sich beklagen †.............to complain
empfehlen *irreg*............to recommend
hassen...........................to hate
reichen..........................to pass
vorziehen *irreg sep* ......to prefer

For **accepting and refusing** see page 59
For **food** see page 52

Phrases

Hast du Durst? *Would you like a drink?*
Gehen wir essen? *Shall we go and eat?*
Ich habe einen Tisch für vier reserviert *I have booked a table for four*
Zahlen, bitte! *The bill, please*
Das habe ich nicht bestellt *It is not what I ordered*
Mein Essen ist kalt *My meal is cold*

2E SERVICES

Auf der Post   At the post office

die Adresse (n)............ address
der Brief (e) .... letter
der Briefkasten (-kästen)...letter box
die Briefmarke (n) .... stamp
der Briefträger (-)......... postman
die Post .... post office; mail
das Postamt (-ämter) .... post office
die Postkarte (n)........... postcard
der Schalter (-)............. counter position
die Telefonkarte (n) ..... phone card

das Formular (e).......... form
die nächste Leerung..... the next collection
das Päckchen (-)........... small parcel
das Paket (e)................ parcel
die Postanweisung (en)......postal order

die postlagernde Sendung .... poste restante
per Einschreiben..........by registered post
per Luftpost ....by air mail
ins Ausland..................(to) abroad
dringend ....urgent
verloren ....lost

anrufen *irreg sep* ....to phone
benutzen † ....to use
einwerfen *irreg sep* ......to post
sich irren......................to make a mistake
die Post zustellen *sep* ...to deliver the post
schicken.......................to send, post
weiterschicken *sep* ....to send on
zählen ....to count

For **phoning** see page 56

Phrases

Wo kann ich eine Telefonkarte kaufen? *Where can I buy a phone card?*
Kann ich von hier faxen? *Can I send a fax from here?*
Kann ich von hier eine E-Mail schicken? *Can I e-mail from here?*
Gibt es Post für mich? *Is there any post for me?*

In der Bank   At the bank

die Bank (en) .... bank
der Geldautomat (en) *wk*...cash machine
der Geldwechsel .... exchange of money
die Kasse.................... till
der Kurs .... rate of exchange
die Sparkasse (n) .... savings bank
die Wechselstube (n) ... bureau de change

das Bargeld .... cash
der Cent .... cent
der Euro .... euro, €
der Franken................. Swiss franc
der Fünfzigeuroschein (e)... 50 euro note

das Geld......................money
das Kleingeld...............change
das Pfund ....£ sterling
der Rappen ....1/100 Swiss franc
die Währung (en) ....currency
das Zweieurostück (e)...2 euro coin

der Ausweis (e) ....ID
der Euroscheck (s)........Eurocheque
das Konto (s) ....account
die Kreditkarte (n)........credit card
die Münze (n)..............coin
der Pass (Pässe) ....passport
die Provision (en).........commission
Prozent ....per cent

der Reisescheck (s).......travellers' cheque	an die Kasse gehen* *irreg*
das Scheckheft (e).........cheque book	..............................to go to the cash desk
die Scheckkarte (n).......cheque card	Provision nehmen *irreg* ...to charge commission
der Schein (e)...............note	umtauschen *sep* ....to change
der Wechselkurs (e)......exchange rate	unterschreiben *irreg insep.* to sign
	wechseln.....................to change
akzeptieren † ....to accept	wert sein* *irreg*...........to be worth
ein Formular ausfüllen *sep* .... to fill in a form	zumachen *sep*..............to close
einen Scheck einlösen † *sep* .. to cash a cheque	

Phrases

Gibt es hier in der Nähe einen Geldautomaten? *Is there a cash machine near here?*
Wo kann ich Geld wechseln? *Where can I change money?*

Zu vermieten   For hire

das Boot (e)..................boat
das Fahrrad (-räder) ......bike
die Kaution ....deposit
das Rad (Räder) ....bicycle

mieten † ....to hire
Unterschreiben Sie hier! ... sign here

Fundsachen   Lost property

die Brille.....................pair of glasses
die Brieftasche (n)........wallet
der Fotoapparat (e) ....camera
die Handtasche (n).......handbag
das Handy (s) ....mobile (phone)
die Kamera (s) ....video camera
der Koffer (-) ....suitcase
das Portemonnaie (s) ....purse
der Regenschirm (e) .....umbrella
der Rucksack (-säcke)...rucksack
das Scheckheft (e)........cheque book
der Schlüssel (-)...........key

die Belohnung (en).......reward
die Beschreibung (en)...description
das Datum (Daten)........date
die Farbe (n) ....colour

das Formular (e) ....form
das Fundbüro (s)...........lost property office
die Gebühr (en) ....fee
die Größe ....size
die Marke (n) ....make, brand

eine Art ....a sort of
Es gibt ... drin..............There is ... in it
verloren ....lost

ausfüllen *sep* ....to fill in (form)
berichten †...................to report
bieten *irreg*..................to offer
fallen lassen *irreg*.........to drop
gehören † (+ Dat)........to belong to
liegen lassen *irreg sep*.. to leave behind
legen...........................to put (down flat)
stecken ....to put (in something)
stehlen *irreg* ....to steal
stellen ....to put (upright)
suchen ....to look for
vergessen *irreg*............to forget
verlieren *irreg* ....to lose
zeigen ....to show

For **days of week** see page 86
For **colours** see page 82
For **materials** see page 64

Phrases

Ich habe meine Tasche verloren *I've lost my bag*

Ich habe sie im Bus liegen lassen *I left it on the bus*

Man hat mir mein Handy gestohlen *My mobile phone has been stolen*

Gehen Sie zur Polizeiwache *Go to the police station*

Wie sieht das Portemonnaie aus? *What does the wallet look like?*

Es ist schwarz und aus Leder *It is black and made of leather*

Krankheiten   Health problems

der Durchfall............... diarrhoea

die Erkältung .... cold

das Fieber.................... fever, high temperature

die Grippe................... flu

der Husten................... cough

die Kopfschmerzen *pl*.. headache

der Schnupfen .... cold

die Seekrankheit .... sea-sickness

der Sonnenbrand .... sunburn

der Sonnenstich .... sunstroke

die Tage *pl* .... period

der Heuschnupfen .... hay fever

die Magenverstimmung .....indigestion

das Symptom (e) .... symptom

verstopft .... constipated

der Insektenstich (e)..... insect sting, bite

die Biene (n) .... bee

die Fliege (n) .... fly

die Mücke (n) .... mosquito

die Wespe (n)............... wasp

sich besser fühlen .... to feel better

sich krank/übel fühlen . to feel ill

sich wohl fühlen .... to feel well

krank werden* *irreg* .... to fall ill

Mir ist kalt .... I'm cold

Mir ist warm .... I'm hot

Mir ist schwindlig........ I'm dizzy

Es tut weh .... It hurts

eine Erkältung haben *irreg*.... to have a cold

Fieber haben .... to have a raised temperature

Halsschmerzen haben........ to have a sore throat

Kopfschmerzen haben....... to have a headache

Magenschmerzen haben .... to have stomachache

Ohrenschmerzen haben ..... to have earache

Rückenschmerzen haben ... to have backache

Zahnschmerzen haben ...... to have toothache

Beim Arzt   At the doctor's
Beim Zahnarzt   At the dentist's

die Behandlung (en) .....treatment

die Gesundheit ....health

die Klinik (en) ....clinic

die Krankheit (en) ....illness

das Medikament (e)......medicine

das Mittel ....remedy

der Patient (en) *wk*.......patient

die Praxis (Praxen).......surgery

das Problem (e)............problem

das Rezept (e) ....prescription

die Sprechstunde (n) ....surgery (times)

der Termin (e) ....appointment

die AOK ....sickness scheme

das Attest (e)................certificate

der E111-Schein (e)......E111

der Gips ....plaster (broken bones)

die Kosten *pl* ....expenses, cost

die Operation (en) ....operation

die Plombe (n).............filling

das Röntgenbild (er) .....X-ray

der Schmerz (en) .... pain
die Spritze (n) .... injection
die Versicherung (en) ... insurance
die Wunde (n) .... wound

einen Termin ausmachen *sep*
.... to make an appointment
behandeln † .... to treat
besuchen † .... to go and see
im Bett bleiben* *irreg* .. to stay in bed
einspritzen † *sep* .... to inject (a drug)
husten † .... to cough
Fieber messen *irreg* ...... to take temperature
stechen *irreg* .... to sting

sich ausruhen *sep* .... to rest
beißen *irreg* .... to bite
beraten *irreg* .... to advise s.o
bluten † .... to bleed
sich erbrechen *irreg* ...... to be sick, vomit
Angst haben *irreg* .... to be afraid
ins Krankenhaus kommen* *irreg*
.... to go into hospital
den Arzt kommen lassen *irreg*
.... to send for the doctor
niesen .... to sneeze
pflegen .... to care for, look after
schwitzen .... to sweat
sich übergeben *irreg insep*
.... to be sick, vomit

verschreiben *irreg* .... to prescribe
zittern .... to shiver

In der Apotheke   At the chemist's
die Antibiotika *pl* .... antibiotics
    Aspirin® .... aspirin®
die Damenbinde (n) ..... sanitary towel
das Dragée (s) .... capsule
das Fieber .... temperature
das Hansaplast® .... plaster, elastoplast®
das Hustenbonbon (s) ... throat sweet
der Hustensaft (-säfte) .. cough mixture
der Löffel (-) .... spoonful
der Saft (Säfte) .... (liquid) medicine
die Salbe (n) .... cream, balm
die Tablette (n) .... tablet
der Tampon (s) .... tampon
der Verband (-bände) ... dressing
das Zäpfchen (-) .... suppository

das Aftershave .... after shave
die Creme .... cream
die Seife .... soap
die Sonnencreme .... sun cream
das Tempotaschentuch® .. tissue
die Tube (n) .... tube
die Watte .... cotton wool
die Zahnpasta .... toothpaste

Phrases

Beim Arzt/Bei der Ärztin *At the doctor's*

Was ist los? *What is the matter?*

Ich fühle mich nicht wohl *I don't feel well*

Können sie mir Schmerztabletten geben? *Can you give me some painkillers?*

Hier haben Sie ein Rezept *Here is a prescription*

Nehmen Sie ein Dragee dreimal am Tag nach dem Essen *Take a capsule 3 times a day, after meals*

Gute Besserung! *Get well soon!*

Beim Zahnarzt/Bei der Zahnärztin *At the dentist's*

Ich habe Zahnschmerzen *I have toothache*

Ich habe eine Plombe verloren *I've lost a filling*

An der Apotheke *At the chemist's*

Haben Sie etwas gegen Schnupfen? *Have you something for a cold?*

Ich habe Fieber *I have a temperature*

Haben Sie etwas gegen einen Sonnenbrand? *Have you anything for sunburn?*

Ich möchte Hustensaft *I would like some cough mixture*

Die Dienstapotheke hat am Sonntagmorgen auf *The duty chemist is open on Sunday morning*

Die Körperteile	**Parts of the body**
der Arm (e)	arm
das Auge (n)	eye
das Bein (e)	leg
der Finger (-)	finger
der Fuß (Füße)	foot
der Hals (Hälse)	throat
die Hand (Hände)	hand
der Kopf (Köpfe)	head
der Magen (-)	stomach
das Ohr (en)	ear
der Rücken (-)	back
der Zahn (Zähne)	tooth
das Gesicht (er)	face
die Gesichtszüge *pl*	features
das Haar (e)	hair
das Kinn (e)	chin
die Lippe (n)	lip
der Mund (Münder)	mouth
die Nase (n)	nose
die Stirn (en)	forehead
die Wange (n)	cheek
die Zunge (n)	tongue
der Bauch (Bäuche)	stomach
die Brust (Brüste)	chest, bust, breast
der Daumen (-)	thumb
der Ellenbogen (-)	elbow
der Fingernagel (nägel)	finger nail
das Fußgelenk (e)	ankle

das Handgelenk (e)	wrist
die Hüfte (n)	hip
das Knie (-)	knee
der Nacken (-)	nape of neck
der Oberschenkel (-)	thigh
die Schulter (n)	shoulder
die Taille (n)	waist
der Zeh (en)	toe
das Blut	blood
das Gehirn (e)	brain
die Haut (Häute)	skin
das Herz (en) *wk*	heart
der Knochen (-)	bone
die Leber (n)	liver
der Muskel (-n)	muscle
die Niere (n)	kidney
die Stimme (n)	voice

Was ist los?   **What's the matter?**

allergisch (gegen + Acc)	allergic (to)
asthmatisch	asthmatic
erkältet	having a cold
gesund	healthy
krank	ill
ungesund	in poor health
unwohl	unwell
zuckerkrank	diabetic
behindert	handicapped
geschwollen	swollen

schwach .... weak
sicher .... certain, sure
wirksam .... effective

sich den Arm brechen *irreg* ... to break one's arm
schlucken .... to swallow
sich in den Finger schneiden *irreg*
.... to cut one's finger
sich das Fußgelenk verstauchen †
.... to sprain one's ankle
sich verbrennen *irreg* ... to burn
sich verletzen † .... to hurt o.s, be injured

Ein Unfall   An accident

der Autounfall (-fälle) .. car accident
das Glatteis .... black ice
die erste Hilfe .... first aid
der Knall .... impact
der Notfall (-fälle) .... emergency
der Notruf (e) .... emergency phone call
der Rauch .... smoke
der Schaden (Schäden) . damage
der Unfall (-fälle) .... accident
die Vorsicht .... caution
das Warndreieck .... warning triangle
der Zusammenstoß (-stöße) ..... collision, pile-up
der Zwischenfall (-fälle) .... incident

das Fahrzeug (e) .... vehicle
der Feuerwehrwagen (-) ..... fire engine
der Krankenwagen (-) .... ambulance

For **means of transport** see page 27

die Adresse (n) .... address
die Aussage (n) .... statement
die Erlaubnis (se) .... permission
der Führerschein (e) ...... driving licence
das Kennzeichen (-) ...... registration number
die Polizei *sing* .... the police
die Polizeiwache (n) ..... police station
das Pusteröhrchen .... breath test device

die Versicherung (en) ... insurance

die Ausrede (n) .... excuse
das Problem (e) .... problem
die Richtung (en) .... direction
das Risiko (Risiken) ..... risk
der Schrei (e) .... shout
die Schuld .... fault
die Sicherheit .... safety
die Verletzung (en) ...... injury
die Vorfahrt .... right of way, priority

die Gefahr (en) .... danger
das Glück .... luck
die Hilfe .... help
der Mut .... courage
das Unglück .... bad luck, accident

Leute   People

der Arzt (Ärzte) .... doctor
der Autofahrer (-) .... car driver
die Feuerwehr .... fire brigade
der Feuerwehrmann (-männer) .. fireman
der Fußgänger (-) .... pedestrian
die Krankenschwester (n) . nurse
der Krankenwagenfahrer (-)
.... ambulance driver
der Motorradfahrer (-) .. motorcyclist
der Passant (en) *wk* ...... passer-by
der Polizist (en) *wk* ...... policeman
der Radfahrer (-) .... cyclist
der Verantwortliche ‡ .. the guilty person
der Zeuge (n) *wk* .... witness
die Zeugin (nen) .... witness

Ist es ernst?   Is it serious?

ängstlich .... anxious
atemlos .... breathless
bewusstlos .... unconscious
dringend .... urgent
ernst .... serious
erschöpft .... exhausted

erstaunlich	surprising	Hilfe!	Help!
lebendig	alive, lively	Meine Güte!	My goodness!
mutig	brave	Mensch!	Man!
im Schock	in shock	Pass auf!	Look out!
schrecklich	terrible	Pech!	Hard luck!
schwer verletzt	badly injured	Verzeihung!	Sorry!
tot	dead		
verletzt	injured	abschleppen *sep*	to tow away
		aufpassen † *sep*	to pay attention
folglich	consequently	bremsen	to brake
langsam	slowly	helfen *irreg* (+ Dat)	to help
schnell	quickly	hupen	to sound the horn
sorgfältig	carefully	schieben *irreg*	to push
unvorsichtig	carelessly	schreien *irreg*	to shout, scream
vorsichtig	carefully	stattfinden *irreg sep*	to take place
vorne	in the front	sterben* *irreg*	to die
zufällig	by chance, accidentally	überfahren *irreg insep*	to run over
		überholen *insep*	to overtake

Ausrufe　　　**Exclamations**

Abgemacht!	OK, agreed!	(sich) verletzen †	to injure (o.s)
Ach!	Oh!	weinen	to cry (weep)
Das macht nichts!	Never mind!	winken	to wave
Feuer!	Fire!	zusammenstoßen* mit (+ Dat) *irreg sep*	
Gute Idee!	Good idea!		to collide with, bump into

Phrases

Es hat einen Unfall gegeben *There has been an accident*

Wo/Wann ist es passiert? *Where/When did it happen?*

Der Unfall ist an der Kreuzung passiert *The accident happened at the crossroads*

Rufen Sie den Notdienst an *Phone the emergency service*

Ich habe eine Panne
My car has broken down

der Notruf (e)	emergency call	der Kühler (-)	radiator
die Panne (n)	breakdown	der Lärm	noise (loud)
der Pannendienst	breakdown service	die Marke (n)	make
		der Motor (en)	engine
der Autoschlüssel (-)	car key	der Reifen (-)	tyre
die Batterie (n)	battery	die Reifenpanne (n)	puncture
die Bremse (n)	brake	der Scheinwerfer (-)	headlight
das Geräusch (e)	noise (quiet-ish)	die Windschutzscheibe (n)	windscreen
		der Auspuff	exhaust pipe
		der Blinker (-)	indicator

das Ersatzrad (-räder)....spare wheel
das Ersatzteil (e) ....spare part
das Gas(pedal) ....accelerator
die Hupe (n).................horn
der Kofferraum (-räume) ..boot
die Kupplung (en) ....clutch
das Lenkrad (-räder)......steering wheel
die Scheibe (n).............window
die Scheibenwischer *pl.* ...windscreen wipers
die Schlussleuchten *pl*..rear lights
der Sicherheitsgurt (e) ..seat belt

anrufen *irreg sep* ....to phone
anspringen* *irreg* ....to start (of engine)
sich beeilen † ....to hurry
funktionieren † ....to work
halten *irreg* ....to stop
kaputt gehen* *irreg* ......to break down
eine Panne haben *irreg*.to break down
platzen* † ....to burst (tyre)
reparieren †.................to fix, repair
warten † auf (+ Acc).....to wait for

An der Tankstelle
At the petrol station

das Benzin ....petrol
der Diesel ....diesel
der Liter.......................litre
das Öl ....oil
　　bleifreies Benzin ....unleaded petrol
　　Super bleifrei.........super unleaded
　　verbleites Benzin....leaded petrol

das Getränk (e) ....drink
die Landkarte (n)..........map
die Luft........................air
der Reifendruck............tyre pressure
der Stand ....level
das Wasser...................water

voll tanken...................to fill up
die Reifen kontrollieren † . to check the tyres

Phrases

Ich habe eine Panne *My car has broken down*
Welche Automarke haben Sie? *What make of car is it?*
Wie ist Ihr Kennzeichen? *What is your registration number?*
Wo stehen Sie genau? *Where are you exactly?*
Ich stehe auf der A3 10 Kilometer südlich von Köln in Fahrtrichtung Frankfurt *I'm on the Autobahn A3, 10 kilometres south of Cologne going towards Frankfurt*

WORK AND LIFESTYLE

3A   HOME LIFE

Die Mahlzeiten   Meals

das Abendessen (-)....... dinner, evening meal
das Frühstück (e).......... breakfast
der Imbiss (-e).............. snack
    Kaffee und Kuchen......afternoon coffee
das Mittagessen (-)....... lunch, midday meal
das Picknick (s)............ picnic

For **foods** see page 52
For **times** see page 86
For **days of the week** see page 86

Zu Hause helfen   Helping at home

den Tisch abräumen *sep* ....to clear the table
abtrocknen † *sep* ....to dry dishes
abwaschen *irreg sep* ....to wash up
im Garten arbeiten † ....to work in the garden
auf Kinder aufpassen † *sep* .... to baby sit

mein Zimmer aufräumen *sep*
   .... to tidy my room
bügeln........................... to iron
den Tisch decken.......... to set the table
fegen............................. to sweep
den Hund spazieren führen
   .... to walk the dog
die Katze füttern........... to feed the cat
Einkäufe machen.......... to do shopping
kochen .... to cook
Hausarbeit machen .... to do housework
mein Bett machen......... to make my bed
den Rasen mähen .... to mow the lawn
putzen † .... to clean
spülen .... to wash up
Staub saugen .... to vacuum
Staub wischen .... to dust
das Auto waschen *irreg*
   .... to wash the car

Phrases

Kann ich Ihnen helfen? *Can I help you?*
Kannst du den Tisch decken? *Can you lay the table?*
Wir essen abends um sechs Uhr *We have our evening meal at 6*

Glückwünsche   Best wishes

Herzlichen Glückwunsch! ....Best Wishes!
Herzlichen Glückwunsch zum Geburtstag!
   .... Happy Birthday!
Ein glückliches neues Jahr!
   .... Happy New Year!
Hals- und Beinbruch! .. Good luck!
Einen schönen Tag noch! .....Have a nice day!
Fröhliche Weihnachten! ....Happy Christmas!
Frohe Ostern! .... Happy Easter!
Ich gratuliere! .... Congratulations!
Viel Spaß! .... Have a good time!

Festtage   Festivals

der Ball (Bälle)............ ball
der Feiertag (e) .... public holiday
der Muttertag .... Mother's Day
die Party (s) .... party

   Allerheiligen........... All Saints (Nov 1st)
   Chanukka .... Chanukah
   Diwali.................... Divali
der Faschingsdienstag ..Shrove Tuesday
der Heiligabend .... Christmas Eve
   Heilige Drei Könige ... Twelfth Night

Id.............................Eid
der Karfreitag...............Good Friday
der Karneval ....Carneval
der erste Mai................May 1st
das Neujahr ....New Year's Day
das jüdische Neujahr.....Rosh Hashana
Ostersonntag...........Easter Day
das Passa ....Passover
Pfingsten................Whitsun
Ramadan................Ramadan
der Rosenmontag.........day before Shrove
                                      Tuesday
der Sabbat....................Sabbath
Silvester.................New Year's Eve
Weihnachten...........Christmas
der erste Weihnachtstag.....Christmas Day

das Feuerwerk ....fireworks
die Geburtstagsparty (s) ...birthday party
das Geschenk (e)..........present
die Karte (n) ....card
das Osterei (er)..............Easter egg
der Weihnachtsbaum (-bäume)
..............................Christmas tree
der Weihnachtsmann ....Father Christmas
der Zug (Züge).............procession

For other **celebrations** see page 68

Leute   People

der Christ (en) *wk*........Christian
der Gott ....God
der Hindu (s) ....Hindu
der Jude (n) *wk*.............Jew
die Jüdin (nen) ....Jewess
der Muslim (s)..............Muslim
die Muslime (n)...........Muslim
der Sikh (s)..................Sikh

Wie war das?   **What was it like?**
Familien-.....................of the family
religiös ....religious

sich amüsieren †..........to have a good time
Freunde besuchen †......to visit friends
Freunde einladen *irreg sep*
.............................to have friends round
essen gehen* *irreg* ....to go to a restaurant
feiern ....to celebrate
gratulieren † (+ Dat).....to congratulate
Musik hören ....to listen to music
organisieren †..............to organise
schenken.....................to give a present

For **opinions** see page 78

3B   HEALTHY LIFESTYLE

Das gesunde Leben
A healthy lifestyle

die Biokost................. organic foods
die Fast Food-Industrie
.... fast food industry
das Fett........................ fat
der Fettgehalt.............. fat content
das Gemüse................. vegetables
das Molkereiprodukt (e)....dairy product
die Nahrung................. food
das Obst .... fruit
die Süßigkeiten *pl*........ sweet things
die Vitamine *pl*........... vitamins

die Aerobik................. aerobics
die Fitness................... fitness
das Fitnessprogramm ... work-out
das Fitnesszentrum....... fitness centre
die Gesundheit............ health
der Schlaf................... sleep
der Vegetarier (-) .... vegetarian

fit .... fit
gesund......................... healthy
vegetarisch................. vegetarian

abnehmen *irreg sep* ..... to lose weight
sich entspannen †........ to relax
Diät machen................ to go on a diet
respektieren †............. to respect
superfit sein* *irreg* ..... to be very fit
sich trainieren † .... to train
sich trimmen .... to keep fit
vermeiden *irreg* .... to avoid

For **opinions** see page 78

Lebensmittel kaufen   Buying food
Bäckereiprodukte   Bakery products

der Berliner (-).............doughnut
das Brot........................bread
das Brötchen (-)...........bread roll
das Graubrot ....brown bread
der Keks (e)................biscuit
der Kuchen (-) ....cake
das Schwarzbrot ....black bread
die Torte (n) ....gateau, flan
das Vollkornbrot ....wholemeal bread

Lebensmittel   Groceries

das Bonbon (s).............sweet
die Butter.....................butter
die Chips *pl* ....crisps
das Ei (er) ....egg
das Eis..........................ice cream
die Flakes *pl* ....cornflakes
der Joghurt (s) ....yoghurt
der Käse.......................cheese
der Reis........................rice
die Suppe (n)...............soup
der Zucker ....sugar

der Essig......................vinegar
die Gewürze *pl*............spices
der Honig....................honey
die Margarine ....margarine
die Marmelade (n)........jam
das Mehl ....flour
die Nudeln *pl*...............pasta, noodles
das Öl...........................oil
die Orangenmarmelade marmalade
der Pfeffer...................pepper (spice)
die Sahne.....................cream
das Salz........................salt
der Senf ....mustard

Die Getränke   **Drinks**
die Cola ....cola
der Fruchtsaft (-säfte) ...fruit juice
der Kaffee ....coffee
die Limonade...............lemonade
die Milch ....milk
die Magermilch ....skimmed milk
die Schokolade ....chocolate
der Tee..........................tea
die Vollmilch................full milk

der Alkohol...................alcohol
das Bier ....beer
der Sekt.........................German champagne
der Wein ....wine

Fleisch   **Meat**
der Braten ....joint, roast meat
die Frikadelle (n) ....rissole
das Hackfleisch.............mince
das Hähnchen................chicken
das Kalbfleisch ....veal
das Kotelett (e)..............chop, cutlet
das Rindfleisch ....beef
der Schinken ....ham
das Schnitzel.................escalope
das Schweinefleisch......pork
die Soße (n) ....sauce, gravy
der Speck ....bacon
das Steak (s)..................steak
die Wurst (Würste).......sausage, salami, pâté

die Ente (n)...................duck
das Geflügel ....poultry
das Hammelfleisch ....mutton
das Hirschfleisch...........venison
das Lammfleisch...........lamb
der Truthahn (-hähne)...turkey

Gemüse   **Vegetables**
die (grüne) Bohne (n) ...(green) bean
die Erbsen *pl*................peas

die Gurke (n)................cucumber; gherkin
die Karotte (n)..............carrot
die Kartoffel (n) ....potato
der Kohl ....cabbage
der Kopfsalat...............lettuce
der Pilz (e)...................mushroom
der Salat ....salad; lettuce
die Tomate (n)..............tomato

der Blumenkohl............cauliflower
der Rosenkohl *no pl* .....Brussels sprout(s)
der Rotkohl...................red cabbage
das Sauerkraut ....pickled cabbage
der Spargel ....asparagus
der Spinat ....spinach
die Zucchini *pl* ....courgettes
der Mais ....sweetcorn
die Zwiebel (n)............onion

die Aubergine (n).........aubergine
die rote Beete (n).........beetroot
der Brokkoli ....broccoli
der Champignon (s)......type of mushroom
der Knoblauch ....garlic
der Kohlrabi (s) ....kohlrabi
der rote/grüne Paprika..red/green pepper
der Porree (s)...............leek
das Radieschen (-) ....radish

Obst   **Fruit**
der Apfel (Äpfel)..........apple
die Apfelsine (n) ....orange
die Banane (n).............banana
die Erdbeere (n) ....strawberry
die Himbeere (n) ....raspberry
die Orange (n) ....orange
die Weintraube (n) ....grape

die Ananas (-)..............pineapple
die Birne (n)................pear
die Grapefruit (s).........grapefruit
die Kirsche (n) ....cherry

die Nektarine (n)......... nectarine
die Pampelmuse (n)..... grapefruit
der Pfirsich (e)............ peach
die Pflaume (n)........... plum; prune
die Zitrone (n)............. lemon

die Aprikose (n)........... apricot
die Brombeere (n)........ blackberry
die rote Johannisbeere (n).redcurrant
die schwarze Johannisbeere (n)
.... blackcurrant
die Kiwi (s)................. kiwi
die Mandarine (n)........ tangerine
die Melone (n)............ melon
die Nuss (Nüsse).......... nut
die Stachelbeere (n)..... gooseberry

Fisch   **Fish**
die Fischstäbchen *pl* .... fish fingers
die Forelle (n)............. trout
der Hering (s).............. herring
der Kabeljau................ cod
der Karpfen (-)............ carp
der Lachs.................... salmon
der Räucherlachs.......... smoked salmon
der Schellfisch .... haddock
die Scholle (n) .... plaice
der Thunfisch (e) .... tuna

der Hummer (-)........... lobster
die Krabbe (n)............. shrimp
der Krebs (e) .... crab
die Muscheln *pl* .... mussels

Wie ist es?   **What is it like?**
Bio-........................... organic
hausgemacht .... home-made
lecker .... delicious
natürlich.................... natural

bitter.......................... bitter
frisch .... fresh, not frozen
gewürzt .... spicy

gut durchgebraten .... well-cooked (roast/fried)
roh .... raw
salzig .... salty; savoury
sauer .... sour
scharf.......................... sharp; spicy
süß .... sweet

Rezepte   **Recipes**
auf kleiner Flamme ...... on a low heat
bei mäßiger Hitze .... in a moderate oven
gebraten .... fried, roast
gebuttert .... buttered
gegrillt .... grilled, barbecued
gehackt .... minced
gekocht .... boiled
gerieben .... grated
gewürzt....................... spicy
gut.............................. thoroughly
paniert........................ breaded
roh .... raw, uncooked

die Zutaten *pl* .... ingredients
die Gewürze *pl* .... spices
der Knoblauch .... garlic
die Petersilie............... parsley
der Pfeffer................... pepper (spice)
das Salz....................... salt
der Schnittlauch........... chives

das Basilikum .... basil
der Ingwer .... ginger
der Kümmel................. caraway
der Rosmarin .... rosemary
die Salbei.................... sage
der Thymian .... thyme
der Zimt...................... cinnamon

backen *irreg* .... to bake
braten *irreg*................. to fry, roast
füllen .... to fill, stuff
gießen *irreg* .... to pour
kochen .... to cook, boil

mischen.........................to mix
rollen.............................to roll
schälen..........................to peel
schlagen *irreg*...............to beat
schneiden *irreg*.............to cut
vorbereiten † *sep* ....to prepare

abschmecken *sep* ....to flavour
bräunen.........................to brown, fry gently
kochen lassen *irreg*.......to bring to the boil
würzen † ....to season
zerschneiden *irreg*........to cut up
zudecken *sep* ....to cover

Man braucht ...   **You need ...**
einen Kaffeelöffel.........a teaspoonful
einen Esslöffel ....a tablespoonful
eine Prise ....a pinch of

Maße und Gewichte   **Weights and measures**
die Büchse (n) ....tin
die Dose (n)...................tin, can
die Flasche (n)..............bottle
das Glas.........................jar, pot
der Karton (s)...............cardboard box

die Packung (en) ....packet
die Schachtel (n) ....box
die Tube ....tube
die Tüte (n)...................bag (paper, plastic)

100 Gramm .... 100 grams of
das Gramm .... gram
das Kilo .... kilo
der Liter....................... litre
einen halben Liter .... half a litre of
das Pfund..................... 500 g, pound (lb)
ein halbes Pfund........... 250 g, half a pound

ein bisschen................. a little
ein Dutzend.................. dozen
ein paar......................... a few
ein Paar (e).................. a pair
die Scheibe (n) .... slice
das Stück .... piece; item

die Hälfte (n)............... half
das Drittel .... third
das Viertel .... quarter

For **opinions** see page 78

3C   PART-TIME JOBS, WORK EXPERIENCE

Am Telefon   Phoning

am Apparat .... "speaking", on the phone

Warten Sie auf das Freizeichen!
.... Wait for the dialling code

Bitte, warten Sie! .... Hold the line

besetzt .... engaged, busy

falsch verbunden .... wrong number

außer Betrieb .... out of order

der Anrufbeantworter (-)...answering machine

das Faxgerät (e)............ fax machine

das Handy (s) .... mobile phone

der Hörer (-)................. handset

das Kartentelefon (e).... card phone

das Münztelefon (e) ..... payphone

die Telefonkarte (n) ..... phonecard

die Telefonzelle (n) ..... phone box

der Anruf (e) .... phone call

der Anrufer (-) .... caller

die Auskunft .... directory enquiries

die E-Mail-Adresse...... e-mail address

die Faxnummer (n) ...... fax number

das Freizeichen .... dialling tone

die Münze (n) .... coin

der Notruf (e)............... emergency call

die Nummer (n)........... number

der Tarif (e) .... rate, charge

das Telefonbuch (-bücher) directory

die Vorwahl (en) .... code

die Zahl (en)................ figure, number

die Zentrale .... exchange, operator

den Hörer abnehmen *irreg sep*
.... to lift the handset

anrufen *irreg sep* .... to phone (someone)

den Hörer auflegen *sep*...... to hang up

faxen............................ to fax

klingeln........................ to ring (of phone)

am Telefon sein* *irreg* ...... to be on the phone

sprechen *irreg* .... to speak, talk

telefonieren † .... to phone (in general)

verbinden *irreg*............ to connect

wählen .... to dial

zuhören *sep* .... to listen

zurückrufen *irreg sep* ...to call back

For **times** see page 86

For **duration of time** see page 86

For **transport** see page 27

For **professions** see page 4

Phrases

Ich möchte **Herrn** Braun sprechen *I would like to speak to Mr Braun*

Wann soll ich wieder anrufen? *What time shall I ring back?*

Ich rufe um zwölf Uhr zurück *I'll ring back at midday*

Können Sie Frau Meyer etwas ausrichten? *Can I leave a message for Frau Meyer?*

Darf ich Ihnen meine Telefonnummer geben? *May I leave my phone number?*

Auf Wiederhören! *Goodbye!*

Samstagsjobs   Saturday jobs

die Arbeit (en) .... work

das Babysitten .... baby sitting

der Job (s) .... job (for student)

der Supermarkt (-märkte) ... supermarket

der Teilzeitjob (s) .... part-time job

der Arbeitgeber (-)........ employer

der Arbeitnehmer (-).....employee

die Arbeitnehmerin (nen) . employee
die Babysitterin (nen) ...babysitter
der Kassierer (-)............till operator
die Kassiererin (nen) ....till operator
der Kellner (-)..............waiter
die Kellnerin (nen) ....waitress
der Praktikant (en)........trainee
die Praktikantin (nen)...trainee
der Verkäufer (-)...........sales assistant
die Verkäuferin (nen) ...sales assistant

Geld ausgeben *irreg sep* ...to spend money
Geld sparen..................to save money
Geld verdienen † ....to earn money

im Monat ....per month
pro Stunde ....per hour
pro Woche ....per week

arbeiten † ....to work
bei Aldi arbeiten † ....to work at Aldi
im Büro arbeiten † ....to work in an office
im Supermarkt arbeiten †
.....................to work in the supermarket
austragen *irreg sep* ....to deliver (newspapers)
Feierabend haben *irreg*.to finish the day's work
die Stellenanzeigen lesen *irreg*
.... to read the job ads
ein Praktikum machen ..to do work experience
Arbeit suchen...............to look for work

Vorteile und Nachteile
Advantages and disadvantages

die Arbeit am Fließband .. assembly line work
die Arbeit im Freien.....outdoor work
die Arbeitszeit.............hours of work
eine Arbeit im Sitzen ...a sitting down job
die Büroarbeit ....office work

gefährlich ....dangerous
langweilig....................boring
schlecht bezahlt............badly paid

abends arbeiten † ....to work evenings
draußen arbeiten † ....to work outdoors
drinnen arbeiten † ....to work indoors
ganztags arbeiten †.......to work full-time
halbtags arbeiten † ....to work part-time
mit Computer arbeiten † .. to use a computer
Tag und Nacht arbeiten †
.... to work day and night
am Wochenende arbeiten †
.... to work weekends
forschen........................to do research
Kontakt mit Leuten haben *irreg*
...................to have contact with people
Leuten helfen *irreg* ......to help people
(ins Ausland) reisen* † ....to travel (abroad)
Erfahrungen sammeln
....................to broaden one's experience
isoliert sein* *irreg*........to be isolated
selbständig sein* *irreg*.to work for oneself
Uniform tragen *irreg*....to wear a uniform
reich werden* *irreg*......to get rich

Phrases

Jeden Samstagmorgen arbeite ich drei Stunden *I work for three hours every Saturday morning*

Vor zwei Monaten habe ich ein Berufspraktikum in einer Fabrik gemacht *Two months ago I did work experience in a factory*

Es ist schwer, einen Job zu finden *It's hard to find a job*

3D LEISURE

Im Fernsehen   On TV

die Dokumentarsendung (en) ... documentary
das Interview (s) .... interview
die Nachrichten *pl* .... news
das Nachrichtenmagazin ...news show
das Programm (e) .... channel
die Reklame (n) .... advert
die Seifenoper (n) .... soap opera
die Sendung (en) .... programme
die Serie (n) .... series
die Sportsendung (en).. sports programme
die Tagesschau .... news
die Wettervorhersage (n) ..weather forecast

die Krimiserie (n) .... police series
die Quizsendung (en)... quiz show
die Talkshow (s) .... a talk show
das Theaterstück (e) ..... play

die Fernbedienung .... remote control
das Kabelfernsehen ...... cable TV
das Digitalfernsehen .... digital TV
der DVD-Spieler (-) ..... DVD player
das Satellitenfernsehen ......satellite TV
die Satellitenschüssel (n) ...satellite dish
die Videokassette (n) ... video cassette
der Videorekorder (-) ... video recorder

der Komödiant (en) *wk* .....comedian
die Komödiantin (en)... comedienne
der Moderator (en)....... presenter
der Schauspieler (-) ...... actor
die Schauspielerin (nen) ...actress
der Zuschauer (-) .... viewer

For **opinions** see page 78

Die Musik   Music

die klassische Musik.... classical music
der Jazz .... jazz

die Popmusik............... pop music
der Rap .... rap
der Rock .... rock
der Schlager (-)............. hit song (in German)

die CD (s) .... compact disc, CD
der CD-Spieler (-) ....CD player
der Kassettenrekorder (-)....... cassette recorder
die Stereoanlage (n) .... stereo system
der Walkman® (s)........ walkman ®

die Band (s) .... group, band
die Gruppe (n) .... group
der Sänger (-)................ singer
die Sängerin (nen) .... singer

anmachen *sep* .... to switch on
aufnehmen *irreg sep*..... to record
ausmachen *sep*............. to switch off
es handelt sich um .... it is about
lachen .... to laugh
schätzen .... to appreciate
zuhören *sep* .... to listen (to)
zusehen *irreg sep* .... to watch

For **music** also see page 9

Im Kino   At the cinema

die Eintrittskarte (n) ..... ticket
der Film (e).................. film
die Nachmittagsvorstellung (en)
.... afternoon performance
die Vorstellung (en) ..... (film) showing

der Charakter (e).......... character
der Held (en) *wk* .... hero
die Heldin (nen) .... heroine
der Kuss (Küsse) .... kiss
der Schurke (n) *wk* .... villain
der Star (s) .... filmstar

Was gibt es?   What's on?

der Abenteuerfilm (e) ...adventure film
der Gruselfilm (e) ....horror film
der Horrorfilm (e) ....horror film
die Komödie (n) ....comedy film
der Krimi (s) ....detective film
der Liebesfilm (c) ....love film
der Science-Fiction-Film (e)
    ....science fiction film
der Spielfilm (e)............feature film
der Spionagefilm (e) .....spy film
der Thriller (s) ....thriller
der Western (s) ....Western
der Zeichentrickfilm (e).....cartoon

im Originalton ....original soundtrack
mit Untertiteln ....subtitled
synchronisiert ....dubbed

Das Theater   The theatre

das Ballett (e)...............ballet
die Bühne (n)................stage (drama)
das Drama (Dramen).....drama
die Garderobe (n) ....cloakroom
die Handlung (en).........plot
die Komödie (n) ....comedy
die Oper (n) ....opera
die Pause (n)................interval
das Publikum ....audience
die Rolle (n).................role
das Theaterstück (e)......play
die Tragödie (n)............tragedy
die Truppe (n)..............theatre company
die Vorstellung (en)......performance

im Parkett ....in the stalls
im ersten Rang........in the circle

Wann ist es?   When is it?

jährlich..........................annually
monatlich.....................monthly
täglich ....daily

wöchentlich ....weekly
am Wochenende...........at the weekend

Wie ist es?   What is it like?

aufregend.....................exciting
außergewöhnlich ....extraordinary
echt gut........................super
eindrucksvoll...............impressive
einmalig ....superb
hervorragend ....excellent
lächerlich.....................ridiculous
langweilig....................boring
nutzlos.........................useless
schlimm........................bad
schrecklich ....awful
seltsam ....funny (odd)
sensationell..................sensational
spannend ....exciting
super............................very good, super
widerlich ....revolting

berühmt ....famous
komisch........................funny, amusing
tragisch........................tragic

Ausgehen   Going out

Willst du mitkommen?
    Do you want to come with me?
die Begegnung (en)......chance meeting
die Einladung (en)........invitation
das Treffen (-)..............meeting
der Treffpunkt ....meeting place
der Vorschlag (-schläge) .. suggestion

For **times** see page 86
For **days of the week** see page 86

Annehmen   Accepting

Abgemacht ....OK, agreed
Danke ....Thank you
Es kommt darauf an .....It depends
gern ....with pleasure, gladly

gut .... good
natürlich .... of course
in Ordnung .... OK
sicher .... certainly

Ablehnen   **Refusing**
Es geht nicht, weil ... ... It's impossible,
                             because ...
Es tut mir Leid, aber ... .Sorry, but ...
Leider ... . I'm afraid ...
Ich kann nicht .... I can't
Ich bin verabredet .... I'm not free

nein, danke .... no thank you
leider .... unfortunately

Treffpunkte   **Meeting places**
das Café (s) .... café
die Disco (s) .... disco
die Eisbahn (en) .... ice rink
das Eiscafé (s) .... ice cream parlour
das Freibad (-bäder) ..... open air swimming pool
das Geschäft (e) .... shop
das Hallenbad (-bäder). indoor swimming pool
das Kino (s) .... cinema
der Laden (Läden) .... shop
der Nachtklub (s) .... nightclub
der Park (s) .... park
die Party (s) .... party (celebration)
das Spiel (e) .... match
das Sportzentrum (-zentren)... sports centre
das Theater .... theatre

Wo treffen wir uns?   **Where shall we meet?**
an der Bushaltestelle .... at the bus stop
am Bahnhof .... at the station
im Café .... in the café
im Restaurant .... in the restaurant
in der Disco .... in the disco
vor dem Kino .... outside the cinema

begleiten † .... to go with
besuchen † .... to go and see

einladen *irreg sep* .... to invite
entscheiden *irreg* .... to decide
sich verabreden † .... to arrange to meet
stattfinden *irreg sep* ..... to take place
treffen *irreg* .... to meet
vorschlagen *irreg sep* ... to suggest
warten auf † (+ Acc) .... to wait for

Eintrittskarten kaufen   **Buying tickets**
der Eintritt (e) .... entrance (price)
die Eintrittskarte (n) ..... ticket
der Eintrittspreis (e) ...... entrance (cost)
die Ermäßigung (en) ..... reduction
der Platz (Plätze) .... seat
der Preis (e) .... cost, price
die Schülerermäßigung ..... school student rate
der Sitz (e) .... seat
im voraus .... in advance

der Erwachsene (n) ‡ .... adult
das Kind (er) .... child
der Schüler (-) .... school student
die Schülerin (nen) .... school student
der Student (en) *wk* ...... university student
die Studentin (nen) .... university student

Öffnungszeiten   **Opening times**
Geschäftszeiten .... opening hours
an Feiertagen .... on bank holidays
um ein Uhr .... at one o'clock

eine halbe Stunde .... half an hour
die Stunde (n) .... hour, sixty minutes

geschlossen .... closed
geöffnet .... open
von 9 Uhr bis 12 Uhr.... from 9.00 till 12.00

Das Spiel   **The game**
der Anfang .... start, beginning
der Beginn .... start, beginning
die Niederlage (n) .... defeat

der Sieg (e) .... win
das Tor (e)..................... goal
unentschieden spielen ... to draw

viele Leute .... lots of people
die Mannschaft (en)...... team
der Schiedsrichter (-) .... referee
der Spieler (-)............... player
der Torwart (e)............. goalkeeper
der Zuschauer (-) .... spectator
die Zuschauer *pl* .... crowd

aufregend .... exciting
fair .... fair
unfair .... unfair

gewinnen *irreg* .... to win
schlagen *irreg* .... to beat
teilnehmen an (+ Dat) *irreg sep*
.... to take part in
verlieren *irreg*.............. to lose

For **sport** see page 7

Die Lektüre   **Reading**
der Artikel (-)............... article
der Bericht (e).............. report
das Buch (Bücher) .... book
das Ende....................... end

die Handlung............... plot
der Held (en) *wk*........... hero
die Heldin (nen) .... heroine
die Illustrierte (n) ‡ ...... illustrated magazine
die Leidenschaft (en).... passion
die Modezeitschrift (en)... fashion magazine
die Rolle (n) .... role
der Roman (e) .... novel
die Seite (n)................. page
das Tagebuch (-bücher) diary
die Tageszeitung (en)... daily paper
das Taschenbuch (-bücher) paperback
das Thema (Themen).... theme
die Umfrage (n)........... survey
die Zeitschrift (en) .... magazine
die Zeitung (en)........... newspaper

eine Art .... a sort of
das Ding (e) .... thing
das Dingsbums .... a thingummyjig
der Eindruck (e) .... impression
der Typ (en)................. type, fellow

Es handelt sich um… ... It's about …
wünschen .... to wish
vorschlagen *irreg sep*... to suggest

For **opinions** see page 78

3E SHOPPING

Allgemeines   General
das Einkaufen .... shopping
die Einkaufsliste (n)..... shopping list
das Einkaufszentrum (-zentren)
.... shopping centre
das Geschäft (e) .... shop
der Laden (Läden)........ shop
die Stadtmitte (n)......... town centre
der Stadtrand (-ände).. outskirts

Leute   People

der Händler (-) .... shopkeeper
die Händlerin (nen)...... shopkeeper
der Kassierer (-)........... cashier
die Kassiererin (nen) ... cashier
der Kunde (n) *wk* .... customer
die Kundin (nen).......... customer
der Geschäftsführer (-). manager
die Geschäftsführerin (nen) ... manager
der Verkäufer (-).......... sales assistant
die Verkäuferin (nen) .. sales assistant

Die Geschäfte   The shops

die Apotheke (n).......... chemist's shop
(dispensing)
die Bäckerei (en).......... baker's shop
die Drogerie (n) .... chemist's shop
(non-dispensing)
die Fleischerei.............. butcher's shop
der Friseursalon (s)...... hairdresser's salon
das Kaufhaus (-häuser) .....department store
die Konditorei (en) ...... cake shop, sweet shop
das Lebensmittelgeschäft (e).. grocer's shop
die Metzgerei (en) .... butcher's shop
der Supermarkt (-märkte) ...... supermarket
der Zeitungsstand (-stände).... news stand

die Buchhandlung (en) .... bookshop
das Delikatessengeschäft (e).. delicatessen
die Gemüsehandlung (en)...... greengrocer's

das Kleidergeschäft (e).clothes shop
der Markt (Märkte).......market
die Obsthandlung (en)..fruit seller's
die Reinigung ....dry cleaner's

die Eisenwarenhandlung (en)
................................ironmonger's shop
das Fischgeschäft (e) ....fish shop
das Fotogeschäft (e)......photographer's
das Juweliergeschäft (e) ... jeweller's shop
der Optiker (-) ....optician
das Reisebüro (s) ....travel agency
das Schreibwarengeschäft (e)
................................stationer's shop
der Tabakwarenladen (-läden)
................................tobacconist's shop
der Tante-Emma-Laden (Läden)
.... convenience store, corner shop
das Warenhaus (-häuser) .. department store

Im Geschäft   In the shop
das Erdgeschoss............ground floor
die Etage (n).................storey
das Geschoss (-e)..........floor
der Eingang (-gänge)....entrance
der Stock (Stockwerke) ... floor
der oberste Stock ....top floor
das Untergeschoss ....basement

die Abteilung (en) ....department
der Aufzug (-züge) ....lift
die Ausstellung (en) .....display
der Einkaufswagen (-) ..trolley
der Fahrstuhl (-stühle)..lift
der Fensterladen (-läden).... shop window
die Kasse (n)................cash desk
der Korb (Körbe)..........basket
die Rolltreppe (n) ....escalator
das Schaufenster (-)......shop window
die Umkleidekabine (n)... changing room

der Artikel (-)................article
das Etikett (en)..............label
die Marke (n)................make, brand
der Preis (e) ....price
das Produkt (e).............product
die Qualität (en)............quality
die Quittung (en) ....receipt
die Waren *pl* ....goods

das Handy (s) ....mobile phone
die Klamotten *pl (coll)*.clothes, stuff
die Kleider *pl* ....clothes
das Mountainbike (s)....mountain bike
die Turnschuhe *pl* ....trainers
das Videospiel (e)........video-game
der Walkman® (s)........personal stereo
die Zeitschrift (en) ....magazine

Schilder   Signs

Achtung!......................Attention! Look out!
Ausgang.......................exit
Ausverkauf ....sale
ausverkauft ....sold out
Drücken ....push
Eingang........................entrance
geöffnet........................open
geschlossen...................closed
Notausgang..................emergency exit
Öffnungszeiten *pl* ....opening hours
reduziert.......................reduced
Ruhetag........................rest day
Schlussverkauf ....sale
Selbstbedienung ....self-service
Sonderangebot ....on special offer
Ziehen...........................pull
zu verkaufen ....for sale

an der Kasse bezahlen ..pay at the cash desk
aus zweiter Hand ....second-hand
bitte nicht berühren.......please do not touch
hier erhältlich...............on sale here
Preisknüller..................fantastic prices
Preisnachlass ....reductions

Sachen kaufen   Buying things

die CD (s) ....CD
der Computer (-)..........computer
die DVD (s) ....DVD
die Ferien *pl*................holidays
das Geschenk (e)..........present

Kleidung kaufen   Buying clothes

der Badeanzug (-züge) . swimsuit
die Badehose (n) ....swimming trunks
die Bluse (n)................blouse
das Hemd (en) ....shirt
die Hose (n).................pair of trousers
die Jacke (n).................jacket
die Jeans......................pair of jeans
der Hut (Hüte) ....hat
das Kleid (er)...............dress
die Krawatte (n) ....tie
der Mantel (Mäntel) .....coat, overcoat
die Shorts *pl* ....pair of shorts
der Pullover (-)............pullover
der Pulli (s) *coll*...........pullover
der Rock (Röcke) ....skirt
der Schlips (e) ....tie
das Sweatshirt (s) ....sweatshirt
das T-Shirt (s)...............T-shirt
der Trainingsanzug (-züge) ....tracksuit

der Hausschuh (e).........slipper
ein Paar ... .a pair of ...
der Pantoffel (n) ....slipper
die Sandale (n) ....sandal
der Schuh (e) ....shoe
die Socke (n) ....sock
der Stiefel (-) ....boot
die Turnschuhe *pl* ....trainers

der Bademantel (-mäntel).. dressing gown
der BH (s)....................bra
das Nachthemd (en)......nightdress

der Schlafanzug (-anzüge) .. pyjamas
der Slip (s) .... knickers
die Strumpfhose (n) ..... tights
die Unterhose (n) .... underpants
die Unterwäsche .... underwear

der Bikini (s) .... bikini
der Gürtel (-) .... belt
die Mütze (n) .... cap, hat
der Handschuh (e) .... glove
der Regenmantel (-mäntel) .... raincoat

der Anzug (Anzüge) .... suit (man)
das Kostüm (e) .... suit (woman)
der Schal (s) .... scarf
die Weste (n) .... waistcoat

das Armband (-bänder) ......bracelet
die Armbanduhr (en) ... watch
der Ärmel (-) .... sleeve
die Gürteltasche (n) ..... bumbag, pouch
die Halskette (n) .... necklace
der Knopf (Knöpfe) ..... button
der Kragen (-) .... collar
die Ohrringe *pl* .... earrings
der Regenschirm (e) ..... umbrella
der Reißverschluss (-schlüsse) ....zip
der Ring (e) .... ring
der Schmuck .... jewellery
die Tasche (n) .... pocket; bag
das Taschentuch (-tücher) ... handkerchief

Material   **Material**

aus Baumwolle .... made of cotton
aus Gold .... made of gold
aus Gummi .... made of rubber
aus Holz .... made of wood
aus Kunststoff .... made of plastic
aus Leder .... made of leather
aus Metall .... made of metal
aus Seide .... made of silk
aus Silber .... made of silver
aus Stoff .... made of cloth
aus Wolle .... made of wool

Make-up   **Make-up**

der Lidschatten .... eye shadow
der Lippenstift (e) .... lipstick
die Mascara .... mascara
der Nagellack .... nail varnish
das Parfüm .... perfume
die Schminke .... make-up
sich schminken .... to put on make-up

Allgemeines   **General**

die Mode (n) .... fashion
die Größe (n) .... size
der Stil (e) .... style

Welche Größe?   **What size is it?**

klein .... small
mittelgroß .... medium
groß .... large
Größe 40 .... size 12

Welche Schuhgröße haben Sie?
What size shoes do you take?

Größe 38 .... size 5
Größe 42 .... size 8

Wie ist es?   **What is it like?**

dunkel .... dark (colour)
gestreift .... striped
hell .... light (colour)
kostbar .... valuable
uni *inv* .... plain coloured

For **colours** see page 82

ähnlich .... similar
aus zweiter Hand .... second hand
billig .... cheap
gratis .... free
günstig .... good value (of prices)
kostenlos .... free
preiswert .... cheap, good value
verschieden .... different

modisch ....fashionable
unmodisch ....unfashionable
etwas Billigeres ....something cheaper
zu eng ....too tight
zu groß..........................too big
zu kurz ....too short
zu teuer ....too expensive
zu weit ....too big

Bezahlen   **Paying**
die Brieftasche (n) ....wallet
der Cent ....cent
der Euro, € ....euro, €
die Euroscheckkarte (n)....Eurocheque card
der 20-Euroschein (e) ...20 euro note
der Franken...................Swiss franc
das Geld ....money
der Geldbeutel (-) ....purse
die Kasse (n)................cash desk, till
das Kleingeld ....change
die Kreditkarte (n) ....credit card
die Münze (n) ....coin
das Portemonnaie (s) ....purse
der Preis (e) ....price
die Quittung (en) ....receipt
das Stück......................per item

Nützliche Verben   **Useful verbs**
anprobieren † *sep* ....to try on
ausgeben *irreg sep*........to spend
zu viel ausgeben ....to spend too much
auswählen *sep*...............to choose
beweisen *irreg*.............to prove
bringen *irreg*................to bring
brauchen ....to need
einwickeln *sep* ....to wrap up, gift wrap
falten † ....to fold
messen *irreg* ....to measure
knapp bei Kasse sein* *irreg* ....to be broke
versprechen *irreg*..........to promise
vorschlagen *irreg sep* ...to suggest
vorziehen *irreg sep*.......to prefer

wiegen *irreg*................to weigh
zurückkommen* *irreg sep* .....to come back

bezahlen † ....to pay, pay for
die Quittung behalten *irreg*
          ....to keep the receipt
prüfen ....to check
rechnen † ....to add
Das reicht ....That's enough
schulden † ....to owe
zusammenrechnen † *sep* .. to add up

Was funktioniert nicht?
What is broken/not working?

die Armbanduhr (en).... watch
der CD-Spieler (-) .... CD player
der Computer (-) .... computer
der Fotoapparat (e)....... camera
die Spülmaschine (n) ... dishwasher
die Taschenlampe (n)... torch
die Waschmaschine (n) washing machine

Beschwerden   **Complaints**
die Batterie (n) .... battery
die Beschwerde (n) ...... complaint
das Leck (s) .... leak
das Loch (Löcher) .... hole
die Reparatur (en) .... repair
die Überschwemmung (en)....flood

eingeklemmt................. jammed, stuck
eingelaufen .... shrunk
enttäuscht .... disappointed
fertig........................... ready
gebrochen.................... broken
gerissen .... torn
kaputt .... broken, not working
praktisch..................... practical
stark............................ strong, solid
verstopft .... blocked
nicht zufrieden .... not satisfied

sich beschweren † .... to complain	kontrollieren † .... to check
brechen *irreg* .... to break	kritisieren † .... to criticise
einlaufen* *irreg sep* ..... to shrink	reinigen lassen *irreg* ..... to have cleaned
ersetzen † .... to replace	reißen *irreg* .... to tear, rip
fallen lassen *irreg* .... to drop	reparieren † .... to mend, repair, fix
funktionieren † .... to work, function	reparieren lassen *irreg* .. to have mended
gewährleisten † .... to guarantee	zurücknehmen *irreg sep* ... to take back

---

Phrases

Ich bin dran *It's my turn*

Haben Sie dieses Hemd in Blau, bitte? *Have you got this shirt in blue, please?*

Was kostet dieser Pullover, bitte? *How much is this pullover, please?*

Es tut mir Leid, aber wir haben keine mehr *I'm sorry we haven't any left*

Ich nehme diese Socken. Ich mag die Farbe *I'll take these socks. I like the colour*

Ich kaufe lieber in Kaufhäusern ein. Die Preise sind niedriger
     I prefer shopping in department stores. The prices are lower

Kann ich mein Geld zurückbekommen? *Can I have my money back, please?*

THE YOUNG PERSON IN SOCIETY

4A   CHARACTER AND PERSONAL RELATIONSHIPS

Der Charakter   Character

die Art (en) ....manner
das Benehmen...............behaviour
das Gefühl (e) ....feeling
der Geist ....mind, spirit
die Gewohnheit (en).....habit
das Glück ....happiness
der Humor....................humour
das Interesse (n) ....interest
der Unterschied (e) ....difference

der Charme ....charm
die Großzügigkeit.........generosity
die Intelligenz..............intelligence
die Freundlichkeit.........kindness
die Neugier ....curiosity
das Selbstbewusstsein...confidence
der Sinn für Humor.......sense of humour
der Stolz.......................pride
die Sympathie...............liking, friendship
die Vorstellungskraft ....imagination

die Arroganz.................arrogance
die Eifersucht ....jealousy
die Faulheit..................laziness
die Schuld (en) ....fault, guilt
die Selbstsucht..............selfishness
die Sorge (n)................care, worry
die Wut........................anger

die Freundschaft (en)....friendship
die Hoffnung (en)........hope
die Liebe (n) ....love
die Lust........................desire
der Optimist (en) *wk*.....optimist
der Pessimist (en) *wk*....pessimist

aktiv.............................active
angenehm ....pleasant

charmant......................charming
ehrlich ....honest
fleißig..........................hard-working
freundlich ....friendly
fröhlich........................happy, cheerful
geduldig.......................patient
glücklich......................happy, pleased
hilfsbereit ....helpful
höflich ....polite
humorvoll....................humorous
komisch.......................funny, amusing
lustig............................amusing
offen ....open, frank
sympathisch.................nice
vernünftig....................sensible
witzig ....witty
zufrieden ....content

ärgerlich ....annoying, annoyed
böse ....angry; naughty; nasty
dumm ....stupid
egoistisch ....selfish
ekelhaft........................disgusting
faul ....lazy, idle
frech ....cheeky
gemein.........................mean, nasty
humorlos ....humourless
nervös..........................nervous
traurig..........................sad
unangenehm ....unpleasant
ungeduldig...................impatient
unglücklich..................unhappy, unfortunate
unhöflich ....impolite

enttäuscht ....disappointed
erstaunt........................surprised, amazed
neugierig ....curious

67

ordentlich .... neat, tidy
ruhig .... calm, quiet
selbständig .... independent
seltsam .... odd, strange
sportlich .... sporty, athletic

ausgeglichen .... balanced
begabt .... gifted
klug .... clever
schlau .... clever, cunning, wily
stolz .... proud
gut erzogen .... well brought up
guter Laune .... in a good mood

deprimiert .... depressed
doof *coll* .... stupid
eifersüchtig .... jealous
launisch .... moody
stur .... obstinate
unausstehlich .... unbearable
verrückt .... mad
verwöhnt .... spoilt (child)
schlechter Laune .... in a bad mood

artig .... well-behaved

empfindlich .... sensitive
ernst .... serious
niedlich .... cute
romantisch .... romantic
schüchtern .... shy
unbeholfen .... clumsy
verliebt (in + Acc) .... in love (with)

aussehen *irreg sep* .... to look (appearance)
beschreiben *irreg* .... to describe
erkennen *irreg* .... to recognise
scheinen *irreg* .... to seem

sich benehmen *irreg* ..... to behave
bewundern .... to admire
Angst haben *irreg* .... to be afraid
kennen lernen *sep* .... to get to know
lieben .... to like, love
plaudern .... to chatter
sich streiten *irreg* .... to quarrel
übertreiben *irreg insep* . to exaggerate

For **opinions** see page 78
For **family** see page 1

Phrases

Ich komme gut mit meiner Schwester aus *I get on well with my sister*
Meine Eltern verstehen mich nicht *My parents don't understand me*
Sie mögen meine Freunde nicht *They don't like my friends*

Feiern   Celebrations

die Geburt (en) .... birth
der Geburtstag (e) .... birthday
die Hochzeit (en) .... marriage ceremony
das Hochzeitsessen ...... reception
der Namenstag (e) .... name day
die kirchliche Trauung. church wedding
die standesamtliche Trauung .... civil ceremony
die Verlobung .... engagement

buchstabieren † .... to spell
erscheinen* *irreg* .... to appear
heiraten † .... to marry
heißen *irreg* .... to be called
nennen *irreg* .... to name
sich scheiden lassen *irreg* .. to get divorced
geboren sein* *irreg* ...... to be born
unterschreiben *irreg insep* .. to sign

For **festivals** see page 50

4B   THE ENVIRONMENT

Haushaltsmüll   Domestic waste

der Abfall......................rubbish
die Aludose (n).............aluminium can
die Batterie (n)..............battery
die Einwegflasche (n)...non-returnable bottle
das Glas (Gläser) ....glass
der Kunststoff (e)..........plastic
das Metall (e)...............metal
der Müll ....domestic waste
das Papier.....................paper
die Pfandflasche (n)......returnable bottle
die Plastiktüte (n) ....plastic bag
die Stahldose (n)...........steel can

chemisch......................chemical
braun...........................brown
grün.............................green
klar...............................clear
Öko-.............................ecological
vergiftet ....poisoned
wiederverwendbar ....re-usable

zerstören † ....to destroy
verschwenden † ....to waste
produzieren † ....to produce

Umweltverschmutzer   Sources of pollution

die Abgase ....exhaust gases
der Brennstoff (e) ....fuel
die Fabrik (en)..............factory
   FCKW ....CFCs
die chemischen Industrien
   ....chemical industries
das Kernkraftwerk (e)...nuclear power station
die Kohle (n) ....coal
das Kraftwerk (e) ....power station
die Ölraffinerie (n) ....oil refinery
der Öltanker (-)............oil tanker

der Ölteppich (e) ....oil slick
die Pestizide (n) ....pesticide
der saure Regen ....acid rain
die Umweltverschmutzung ....pollution
der Verkehr ....traffic

Kern- ....nuclear
chemisch ....chemical
ökologisch ....ecological
schädlich ....harmful
umweltfeindlich .....environmentally damaging
umweltfreundlich ......environmentally friendly

bedrohen † ....to threaten
verschmutzen † ....to pollute

For **opinions** see page 78
For **home** see page 12
For **transport** see page 27

Die Umwelt verbessern   Improving the environment

der Altglascontainer (-) ..... bottle bank
das Altpapier ....recycled paper
der Brennstoff (e) ....fossil fuel
das Recycling ....recycling
öffentliche Verkehrsmittel *pl*
   .... public transport

weniger........................less
mehr ....more

den Schaden in Grenzen halten *irreg*
   ....to limit the damage
sparen ....to save
verwenden † ....to use
wegwerfen *irreg sep* ....to throw away
wiederverwerten † *insep* .. to recycle

Umweltschutz   Conservation

die Auswirkung (en).... effect
die Folge (n) .... consequence
der Grund (Gründe) ..... reason
die Zukunft .... future
der Zuwachs................ increase

die Energie.................. energy
die Erde (n).................. earth
die Natur..................... nature
die Welt .... world
die Fauna (Faunen)...... wildlife, fauna
die Flora (Floren)........ plants, flora
das Insektizid (e)......... insecticide
das Klima (s)............... climate
das Ökosystem (e)........ ecosystem
die Ozonschicht (en).... ozone layer
die Umwelt .... environment
das Unkrautvernichtungsmittel (-)
.... weed-killer
der Wald (Wälder)....... forest
die Dritte Welt............. the Third World
die Wüste (n) .... wilderness, desert

For **countryside** see page 18

anbauen *sep* .... to grow, cultivate
austrocknen † *sep* .... to parch, dry out
pflücken .... to pick
sinken* *irreg*............... to fall (temperature)
steigen* *irreg*.............. to rise (temperature)
zunehmen *irreg sep* ..... to increase

Unglücke   Disasters

der Brand (Brände) ...... fire
die Dürre..................... drought
die Epidemie (n) .... epidemic
das Erdbeben (-).......... earthquake

die Hungersnot .... famine
die Klimaveränderung (en)
.... climate change
die Krise (n) .... crisis
die Lawine (n) .... avalanche
die Not........................ need
das Ozonloch (-löcher) . hole in the ozone layer
die Stadtverschmutzung .... urban pollution
der Treibhauseffekt .... greenhouse effect
die Überschwemmung (en) ... flood
das Waldsterben .... forest dying
die Zerstörung .... destruction

Vom Aussterben bedrohte Arten
Endangered species

der Blauwal (e)............. blue whale
der Delphin (e) .... dolphin
der Eisbär (en) *wk*........ polar bear
der Elefant (en) *wk* ...... elephant
das Elfenbein .... ivory
das Fell .... fur
das Futter .... fodder
das Habitat (e) .... habitat
der Orang-Utan (s) .... orang-utan
der Panda (s)................ giant panda
der Stoßzahn (-zähne) .. tusk

gefährdet..................... in danger
verletzt........................ injured, wounded

atmen † .... to breathe
leben .... to live
leiden *irreg*................. to suffer
retten † .... to save
schützen † .... to conserve, protect
sterben* *irreg* .... to die
töten † .... to kill

4C   EDUCATION

Höhere Bildung   Higher education

das Diplom (e) ....diploma
die Hochschule (n) ....university
das Studentenwohnheim (e)
................................hall of residence
das Staatsexamen (-).....degree
der Student (en) *wk*.......university student
die Studentin (nen) ....university student
das Studium (Studien) ..study
die Universität (en).......university
die Zukunftspläne *pl*.....future plans

Das Schulleben   School life

die Eltern *pl* ....parents
der Jugendliche (n) ‡ ....teenager
der Lehrer (-) ....teacher
die Lehrerin (nen)........teacher
der Schüler (-)..............school student
die Schülerin (nen) ....school student
der Teenager (-) ....teenager

die Klassenarbeit (en)...assessment/class test
die Prüfung (en)...........examination
die Schularbeit.............school work
die Schuluniform ....school uniform

For **school** see page 21

Die Studiumwahl   Choice of study

die kaufmännische Ausbildung
................................business studies
die Informatik...............ICT
die Humanistik ....humanities, classics
die Fremdsprachen ....languages
Jura ....law
die Musik....................music
die Medizin ....medicine
die Naturwissenschaften *pl* ..... science

diskutieren † ....to discuss
erlauben † ....to allow

helfen *irreg* (+ Dat)...... to help
sich interessieren † für .... to be interested in
schwänzen †................ to skive off school
verbessern † .... to improve
vorziehen *irreg sep* ...... to prefer
weitermachen *sep* .... to continue, carry on
wiederholen *insep* .... to revise

For **school subjects** see page 22
For **professions** see page 4

Ein studienfreies Jahr   A gap year

Man kann … .... You can …
Geld verdienen †.......... to earn money
ins Ausland reisen* †... travel abroad
sich das Studieren abgewöhnen † *sep*
..............to get out of the habit of studying
wieder studieren †........ to pick up one's studies

Die Ausbildung   Training

die Ausbildung .... training scheme
die Berufsausbildung ... vocational training
das Berufspraktikum .... work experience
die Lehre (n) .... apprenticeship
die Weiterbildung........ continuing education
die Volkshochschule (n)...evening classes

sich weiter bilden † ...... to continue education
gute Zeugnisse haben *irreg*
.... to have good references
Diplom machen .... to graduate
Staatsexamen machen.. to graduate
berufstätig sein* *irreg*.. to have a job
studieren † .... to read for a degree

Leute   People

der Auszubildende (n) ‡ ...trainee
der Bewerber (-)........... applicant
die Bewerberin (nen) ... applicant
der Lehrling (e) .... apprentice

4D   CAREERS AND FUTURE PLANS

Die Bewerbung   Getting a job

die Ausbildung .... professional training
der Brief (e) .... letter
die Erfahrung (en)........ experience
der Familienname (n) *wk* ...surname
der Familienstand .... family status
das Geburtsdatum .... date of birth
der Geburtsort.............. place of birth
der Lebenslauf .... CV, curriculum vitæ
die Qualifikation (en) .. qualification
die Stelle (n) .... job, post
das Stellenangebot (e).. job offer
das Staatsexamen (-).... degree
die Verantwortung .... responsibility
der Vorname (n) *wk* ..... first name
das Vorstellungsgespräch (e) interview

arbeiten † .... to work
annehmen *irreg sep* ..... to accept
ausgeben *irreg sep* .... to give, hand out
beraten *irreg* .... to advise
bestätigen † .... to confirm
sich bewerben *irreg* ..... to apply
erhalten *irreg* .... to receive
einen Kurs machen ...... to go on a course

Eigenschaften   Qualities

die Geduld .... patience
die Gesundheit............. good health
die Höflichkeit............. politeness
die Intelligenz .... intelligence
die Persönlichkeit (en). personality, character
der Sinn für Humor...... sense of humour

ehrlich .... honest
erfahren....................... experienced
fleißig.......................... hard-working
geduldig .... patient
höflich......................... polite
professionell .... professional

qualifiziert .... qualified
mit Computerkenntnissen .. computer literate

die Teilzeitarbeit (en)... part-time work
die Vollzeitarbeit (en) .. full-time work

fest angestellt............... permanently employed
gut bezahlt .... well-paid
schlecht bezahlt .... badly paid
regelmäßig................... regular, steady
vorübergehend............. temporary

Im Betrieb   Business

die Aufgabe (n) .... task
der Beruf (e) .... career, profession
der Betrieb (e).............. business, firm
die Firma (Firmen)....... firm
das Geschäft (e) .... business
der Handel .... trade
die Möglichkeit (en)..... opportunity
der Plan (Pläne)........... plan
das Team (s) .... team

die Ambition (en)......... ambition
die Arbeitsbedingungen *pl*
.... working conditions
die Aufstiegsmöglichkeiten
.... opportunites for promotion
die Beförderung (en) .... promotion
der Entschluss (-üsse)... decision
die Gehaltserhöhung .... pay increase
der Streik (s)............... strike
die Wahl (en)............... choice
der Wettbewerb (e)....... competition

das Gehalt (Gehälter).... salary
der Lohn (Löhne).......... pay, wages
der Ruhestand.............. retirement
die Sozialabgaben .... national insurance
die Steuern *pl* .... taxes

im Ausland ....abroad
langfristig ....long term
arbeitslos......................out of work

Leuten helfen *irreg*.......to help people
Geld verdienen † ....to earn money
eine Uniform tragen *irreg*...... to wear uniform
mit dem Computer arbeiten † to use a computer

Leute   **People**
NB The feminine version of a profession is not given where it is formed by adding **-in (nen)** to the masculine noun.

der Angestellte (n) ‡ .....employee
der Arbeitnehmer (-).....employee
der Arbeitgeber (-)........employer
der Arbeitslose (n) ‡ .....unemployed person
der Auszubildende (n) ‡ ...apprentice
der Chef (s).................boss
der Direktor (en)..........director, manager
der Geschäftsführer (-) .manager
der Kollege (n) *wk* ....colleague
die Kollegin (nen) ....colleague
der Lehrling (e)............apprentice
die Leitung.................management
das Personal *sing* ....staff
der Personalleiter (-).....personnel director
der Verkaufsleiter (-)
          ....sales and marketing director

pünktlich ankommen* *irreg sep*
          .... to arrive on time
mit Verspätung ankommen* .....to be late
faxen...........................to fax, send a fax
eine E-Mail schicken....to send an e-mail
arbeitslos sein* *irreg*........ to be unemployed
gut gekleidet sein* ....to be well-dressed
gut organisiert sein* .....to be well-organised

Im Büro   **In the office**
Absender/Abs.........sender
der Anrufbeantworter (-)
          .... answering machine
die Besprechung (en) ...meeting
der Computer (-) ....PC, computer
das Fax (-) ....fax
das Faxgerät (e) ....fax machine
die Faxnummer (n) ......fax number
das Formular (e) ....form
das Fotokopiergerät (e)...... photocopier
die Gewerkschaft (en).......union
die Post..............................post, mail
das Telefonbuch (-bücher) phone book
die Telefonnummer (n)..... phone number
der Termin (e) ....appointment
der Terminkalender (-)......diary
der Umschlag (-schläge) ...envelope

For **professions** see page 4
For **ICT** see page 10
For **opinions** see page 78

4E SOCIAL ISSUES

Die Werbung   Advertising

das Fernsehen.............. television
die Illustrierte (n) ‡...... magazine
das Internet.................. internet
der Katalog (e)............ catalogue
die Litfaßsäule (n)........ advertising pillar
das Magazin (e)........... magazine
das Plakat (e).............. poster
das Poster (-) .... poster
das Radio .... radio
die Reklame (n) .... advert, advertising
der Werbespot (s)........ advertising slot
der Werbespruch (-sprüche)
.... advertising slogan
die Zeitschrift (en)....... magazine
die Zeitung (en) .... newspaper

Die Kleinanzeigen   Small ads

die Ferienwohnung (en)....holiday home
die Geburt (en)............. birth
das Haus (Häuser)........ house
die Hochzeit (en) .... marriage (ceremony)
das Mountainbike (s) ... mountain bike
niedrige Preise *pl* ... low prices
das Produkt (e)............ products
das Rad (Räder) .... bike
das Sonderangebot (e) . special offer
der Tod (e) .... death
der Urlaub .... holidays
das Vergnügen .... pleasure
der Verkauf (-käufe) .... sale
der Wagen (-).............. car
der Wert (e)................. value
die Wohnung (en)........ flat

zu verkaufen .... for sale
zu vermieten .... for hire
billiger......................... less expensive
preiswert .... cheap, good value
im Angebot .... on offer

aus zweiter Hand .... second-hand
im Schlussverkauf .... in the sales
der Rabatt (e).............. discount

Junge Leute   People

der Freund (e).............. friend, boyfriend
die Freundin (nen)........ friend, girlfriend
der Jugendliche (n) ‡ .... teenager
der Kamerad (en) *wk* .... friend, mate
die Kameradin (nen)..... friend, mate

Probleme   Problems

die Arbeit .... work
die Arbeitslosigkeit ...... unemployment
das Asyl .... asylum
die Drogen *pl*.............. drugs
der Geldmangel .... lack of money
die Gewalttätigkeit .... violence
der Job (s).................... job (part-time)
die Mode (n)................ fashion
das Nachsitzen .... detention
der Pickel (-)................ spot, zit
die Popmusik............... pop music
das Problem (e)............ problem
der Rassismus.............. racism
die Scheidung (en) .... divorce
das Schikanieren........... bullying
die Schwierigkeit (en) .. difficulty
die Sorge (n)................ care, trouble
der Vandalismus........... vandalism

begabt .... gifted
benachteiligt .... disadvantaged
gelangweilt .... bored
langweilig................... boring
pflicht *inv* .... compulsory
priviligiert................... privileged
schlecht informiert .... ill-informed
schwach (in) .... no good (at)
verärgert .... angry

74

verwöhnt.......................spoilt (child)
weit außerhalb der Stadt
............................a long way out of town

mein Zimmer aufräumen *sep*
...............................to tidy my room
spät aufstehen* *irreg sep*.... to get up late
mit Chris gehen* *irreg* .... to go out with Chris
früh ins Bett gehen* *irreg* .. to go to bed early
spät ins Bett gehen* *irreg*... to go to bed late
im Haushalt helfen *irreg* .... to help in the house
spülen ....to do the washing up
Geld verdienen † ....to earn money

akzeptieren † ....to accept
ärgern............................to annoy
sich ärgern ....to get angry
sich erinnern an † (+ Dat).....to remember
erlauben † ....to allow
erröten* †......................to blush
Spaß haben *irreg* ....to have fun
kritisieren †...................to criticise
sich langweilen ....to be bored
lügen *irreg* ....to lie
sich Sorgen machen......to worry
die Wahrheit sagen ....to tell the truth
sich streiten *irreg*..........to argue, dispute
verstehen *irreg*.............to understand
sich gut verstehen *irreg* mit (+ Dat)
...............................to get on well with

Wohlfahrtsprobleme
Welfare problems

der Alkohol..................alcohol
die Droge (n) ....drug
das Heroin....................heroin (drug)
die Zigaretten *pl* ....cigarettes

Aids ....Aids
der Alkoholismus ....alcoholism
die Betrunkenheit ....drunkenness (habitual)
die Magersucht ....anorexia

die Schwangerschaft .... pregnancy
der Stress......................stress
die Sucht ....addiction (drug)
die Überdosis ....overdose

der Drogensüchtige ‡ ... drug addict
der Junkie (s)...............junkie
der Raucher (-) ....smoker
der Rowdy (s)...............hooligan

arbeitslos ....out of work
betrunken ....drunk
drogenabhängig............drug dependent
drogensüchtig...............drug dependent
magersüchtig ....anorexic
obdachlos ....homeless
übergewichtig...............obese

abnehmen *irreg sep*......to lose weight
schaden † (+ Dat).........to damage (health)
Drogen nehmen *irreg*...to take drugs
Drogen probieren † ......to try drugs
protestieren †...............to protest
rauchen........................to smoke
spucken ....to spit
zunehmen *irreg sep*......to put on weight

Der Druck   **Pressure**
der Elterndruck............parental pressure
der Gruppendruck ....peer pressure
der Leistungsdruck ....pressure to succeed
der Mediendruck ....media pressure
der Notendruck............exam pressure
der Schuldruck ....school pressure

angespannt...................tense
bestürzt........................upset
gestresst.......................stressed out
unter Druck stehen *irreg*
..............................to be under pressure

Das Verbrechen   Crime

die Brutalität .... brutality
der Einbruch (brüche) .. burglary
der Fall (Fälle) .... case
der Ladendieb (e) .... shoplifter
der Mord (e) .... murder
der Streit (e) .... fight, quarrel
der Überfall (Überfälle) .....robbery, mugging

der Dieb (e) .... thief
der Diebstahl .... theft
der Gefangene ‡ .... prisoner
das Individuum .... individual
der Polizist (en) *wk* ..... policeman
der Richter (-) .... judge
der Staatsanwalt .... examining magistrate
der Taschendieb (e) ..... pickpocket
der Täter (-) .... criminal
der Zeuge (n) *wk* .... witness

das Gewehr (e) .... gun
der Revolver (-) .... revolver
die Waffe (n) .... weapon

der Beweis (e) .... proof
die Dummheit (en) .... stupid mistake
die Einzelheit (en) .... detail
die Entdeckung (en)..... discovery
die Erklärung (en) .... explanation
das Gefängnis (se) .... prison
die Geldstrafe (n) .... fine
das Motiv (e) .... reason, motive
der Streit (e) .... argument
der Verdacht .... suspicion
die Wahrheit .... truth
die Zeugenaussage (n) . evidence

brutal .... brutal
gerecht .... just, fair
gesetzwidrig .... illegal

grausam .... cruel
kriminell .... criminal
mysteriös .... mysterious
schuldig .... guilty
unbekannt .... unknown
ungerecht .... unjust
unschuldig .... innocent
unwahr.......................... untrue
unzulässig.................... inadmissible
wahr............................. true

anfallen *irreg sep* .... to attack
angreifen *irreg sep* .... to attack
begehen *irreg* .... to commit
einbrechen* *irreg sep* ... to burgle
entkommen* *irreg*........ to escape
festnehmen *irreg sep* .... to arrest
fliehen* *irreg*.............. to flee
folgen* (+ Dat) .... to follow
lösen .... to solve
sich nähern (+ Dat)....... to approach
stehlen *irreg* .... to steal
untersuchen *insep*........ to investigate
verschwinden* *irreg* .... to disappear

bestrafen † .... to punish
einsperren *sep* .... to lock up
entdecken † .... to discover
erkennen *irreg* .... to identify
merken.......................... to note, notice
schlagen *irreg*.............. to hit
stehen bleiben* *irreg*.. to stand still
überraschen *insep*........ to surprise
untersagen *insep* .... to forbid
verurteilen † .... to pass sentence
sich weigern .... to refuse
zittern .... to shake, shiver
zweifeln....................... to doubt

COUNTRIES, REGIONS, TOWNS

Die Europäische Union (EU)   The European Union

Country	Meaning	Inhabitant	Inhabitant	Adjective
England	*England*	der Engländer(-)	die Engländerin(nen)	englisch
Irland	*Irish Republic*	der Ire(n)	die Irin(nen)	irisch
Nordirland	*N Ireland*	der Ire(n)	die Irin(nen)	irisch
Schottland	*Scotland*	der Schotte(n)	die Schottin(nen)	schottisch
Wales	*Wales*	der Waliser(-)	die Waliserin(nen)	walisisch
Deutschland	*Germany*	der Deutsche(n)	die Deutsche(n)	deutsch
Österreich	*Austria*	der Österreicher(-)	die Österreicherin(nen)	österreichisch
Belgien	*Belgium*	der Belgier(-)	die Belgierin(nen)	belgisch
Dänemark	*Denmark*	der Däne(n)	die Dänin(nen)	dänisch
Spanien	*Spain*	der Spanier(-)	die Spanierin(nen)	spanisch
Finnland	*Finland*	der Finnländer(-)	die Finnländerin(nen)	finnländisch
Frankreich	*France*	der Franzose(n)	die Französin(nen)	französisch
Griechenland	*Greece*	der Grieche(n)	die Griechin(nen)	griechisch
Italien	*Italy*	der Italiener(-)	die Italienerin(nen)	italienisch
Luxemburg	*Luxembourg*	der Luxemburger(-)	die Luxemburgerin(nen)	luxemburgisch
die Niederlande	*Netherlands*	der Niederländer(-)	die Niederländerin(nen)	niederländisch
Portugal	*Portugal*	der Portugiese(n)	die Portugiesin(nen)	portugiesisch
Schweden	*Sweden*	der Schwede(n)	die Schwedin(nen)	schwedisch

Andere Länder   Other Countries

Afrika	*Africa*	der Afrikaner(-)	die Afrikanerin(nen)	afrikanisch
Amerika	*America*	der Amerikaner(-)	der Amerikanerin(nen)	amerikanisch
Australien	*Australia*	der Australier(-)	die Australierin(nen)	australisch
Europa	*Europe*	der Europäer(-)	die Europäerin(nen)	europäisch
Russland	*Russia*	der Russe(n)	die Russin(nen)	russisch
die Schweiz	*Switzerland*	der Schweizer(-)	die Schweizerin(nen)	schweizerisch

Eigennamen   Proper names

die Alpen *pl* ....Alps
   Bayern ....Bavaria
der Bodensee ....Lake Constance
   Brügge ....Bruges
   Brüssel..................Brussels
die Donau ....the Danube
   Genf......................Geneva
der Kanal ....the English Channel
   Köln......................Cologne
   Lüttich ....Liège

das Mittelmeer.............Mediterranean
die Mosel ....the Moselle
   München ....Munich
die Nordsee ....North Sea
die Ostsee...................Baltic Sea
der Rhein....................the Rhine
der Schwarzwald..........the Black Forest
die Themse.................the Thames
   Venedig.................Venice
   Wien.....................Vienna

ESSENTIAL VOCABULARY

Opinions

Was meinst du?	What is your opinion?
Ich mag (nicht)	I (don't) like
Ich mag lieber	I prefer
Das gefällt mir (nicht)	I (don't) like
Ich hasse	I hate
Ich kann … nicht leiden	I can't stand …
Ich bin deiner Meinung	I share your opinion
Ich bin (nicht) einverstanden	I (don't) agree
Du hast Recht/Unrecht	You are right/wrong
Das stimmt	That's right
Ich denke, dass …	I think that ...
Ich glaube ja	I think so
Ich muss gestehen, dass …	I must admit that …
Ich weiß nicht	I don't know
Es ist möglich	It's possible
Es kommt darauf an	That depends
Man sagt, dass ...	They say that …
im Gegenteil	on the contrary
Ich glaube nicht	I don't think so
Ich gebe dir/ihm/ihr/ihnen/Ihnen Schuld …	I blame you/him/her/them/you

Justifications

Ich mag das	I like it
Es ist lustig	It's amusing
Es ist lecker	It's delicious
Es ist einfach	It's easy
Es ist interessant	It's interesting
Es ist faszinierend	It's fascinating
Es ist wunderschön	It's wonderful
Es ist nützlich	It's useful
Er/Sie ist sympatisch/nett	He's nice/She's nice
Es interessiert mich	It interests me
Es amüsiert mich	It amuses me
Es lohnt sich	It's worth it
Ich schwärme für … (+ Acc)	I am keen on …
Es macht mir Spaß	I enjoy it

Ich mag das nicht	**I don't like it**
Es ist kompliziert	It's complicated
Es ist ekelhaft	It's disgusting
Es ist schwierig	It's difficult
Es ist reizend	It's annoying
Es ist langweilig	It's boring
Es ist unglaublich	It's unbelievable
Es ist schrecklich/furchtbar	It's awful

Es ist zu teuer	It's too expensive
Es ist zu kompliziert	It's too complicated
Es ist zu schwierig	It's too difficult
Es ist zu weit	It's too far away
Es ist zu lang/kurz	It's too long/short
Es ist unpraktisch	It's impractical
Es ist unmöglich	It's impossible
Es ist eine Zeitverschwendung	It's a waste of time
Es ist Blödsinn/Quatsch	It's nonsense

Es reizt mich auf	It irritates me
Es ärgert mich	It annoys me
Es geht mir auf die Nerven	It gets on my nerves
Es langweilt mich	It bores me
Es macht mich müde	It makes me tired
Es passt mir nicht	It doesn't suit me
Ich habe kein Geld/keine Zeit	I have no money/no time
Ich habe die Nase voll	I'm fed up with it

Excuses

Entschuldigung!	Sorry, excuse me
Schade!	What a pity
Ich habe das nicht extra gemacht	I didn't do it on purpose
Es tut mir Leid	I am sorry

Neutral comments

Gern geschehen/Nichts zu danken/Bitte	Don't mention it
Das macht nichts	That doesn't matter
Das ist mir egal	I'm not bothered
Machen Sie sich keine Sorgen	Don't worry
Vergessen wir es	Let's forget it
Ich habe keine Ahnung	I haven't the faintest idea

Prepositions

Prepositions + Accusative
bis .... as far as; until
durch .... through
entlang .... along
für .... for
gegen............................ against
ohne .... without
um............................... at (clock times), round; about

Prepositions + Dative
aus............................... out of
außer .... except for
bei .... at, at the house of
gegenüber.................... opposite
mit............................... with
nach............................. to, after (time)
seit .... since, for
von .... from, of
zu .... to, at, for

Prepositions + Dative or Accusative
an .... on, at, of
auf............................... on, at, in
hinter........................... behind
in.................................. in, inside
neben........................... next to
über............................. over, more than
unter............................ under, among
vor............................... in front of, before
zwischen .... between

Prepositions + Genitive
anstatt.......................... instead of
außerhalb .... outside (of)
innerhalb..................... within
statt .... instead of
trotz............................. despite, in spite of
während .... during
wegen.......................... because of

Conjunctions

Co-ordinating conjunctions
und...............................and
aber..............................but
oder..............................or
sondern ....but not
denn.............................for

Subordinating conjunctions
als ....when (1 occasion in past)
bevor............................before
bis ....until
da.................................as
damit............................so that
dass..............................that
nachdem ....after
obwohl.........................although
seitdem ....since
sobald ....as soon as
sodass ....in such a way that
während.......................while, whilst
weil..............................because
wenn ....if, when, whenever
wie...............................as, how

Questions

Seit wann …? ....How long ... for?
Wann? ....When?
Warum?........................Why?
Was?.............................What?
Was für …? ....What sort of ...?
Welcher/Welche/Welches ..... Which?
Wer? ....Who?
Wie? ....How?
Wie lange?....................How long?
Wie bitte? ....Pardon?
Wie ist ...? ....What is ... like?
Wieso?..........................Why?
Wie viel? ....How much?
Wo?..............................Where?
Woher? ....Where ... from?
Wohin? ....Where ... to?

Adjectives

alt	old
billig	cheap
cool	cool, trendy
falsch	wrong, false
furchtbar	terrible
glücklich	pleased, happy
groß	big, great, tall
gut	good
intelligent	intelligent
interessant	interesting
jung	young
kalt	cold
klein	little, small, young
kurz	short
lang	long
langweilig	boring
letzt…	the last, the latest
modern	modern
nett	kind
neu	new
normal	normal
richtig	true
schlecht	bad
schön	fine, handsome
teuer	dear, expensive
toll	great; mad
unglücklich	unhappy, unlucky
warm	hot, warm
wunderbar	wonderful

angenehm	pleasant
arm	poor
artig	well-behaved
ausgezeichnet	excellent
besonder…	special
brav	well-behaved
faul	lazy
fleißig	hard-working
froh	happy, merry
klar	clear, obvious
klasse *inv*	great, terrific

leicht	easy
mies	rotten, ugly, lousy
(un)möglich	(im)possible
müde	tired
nächst…	next
nötig	necessary
prima *inv*	great
ruhig	calm, quiet
schwer	difficult
stark	strong
sympatisch	nice
unangenehm	unpleasant
wichtig	important

ängstlich	anxious
beide	both
bekannt	well-known
beschäftigt	busy
blöd	stupid
erfolgreich	successful
enttäuschend	disappointing
ernst	serious
fabelhaft	fabulous
fantastisch	fantastic, great
genau	exact
gewöhnlich	usual, common
gutaussehend	good-looking
hässlich	ugly
hoch	high
kühl	cool, fresh
laut	noisy
lebhaft	lively, keen
lustig	amusing
riesengroß	enormous
rund	round
sauber	clean
schmutzig	dirty
schwach	weak
traurig	sad
unartig	naughty
zufrieden	content

Colours

blau	blue
bunt	brightly coloured
braun	brown
gelb	yellow
grau	grey
grün	green
lila *inv*	mauve
orange *inv*	orange
rosa *inv*	pink
rot	red
schwarz	black
violett	purple
weiß	white
hellblau	light blue
dunkelblau	dark blue

Adverbs

Common adverbs

also	so, therefore
anders	differently
auch	also, as well, too
bald	soon
bestimmt	definitely
danach	after that
dann	then
eben	just
endlich	finally
ganz	quite, fairly, rather
genug	enough
gern	gladly
gleich	immediately
glücklicherweise	fortunately
gut	well
hoffentlich	hopefully
immer	always, still
jetzt	now
leider	unfortunately
manchmal	sometimes
natürlich	of course
normalerweise	usually, normally
schon	already

sehr	very
sicher	certainly
sofort	at once
sogar	even
viel	a lot
vielleicht	perhaps, maybe
wieder	again
wirklich	really
ziemlich	rather
zu	too
zuerst	first, first of all
zuletzt	at last, finally
zum Beispiel, z.B.	for example, eg
zusammen	together

Adverbs of place

da	there
dort	there
dort drüben	over there
draußen	outside
hier	here
oben	upstairs
überall	everywhere
unterwegs	on the way
unten	downstairs

Adverbs of manner

fließend	fluently
plötzlich	suddenly
schnell	quickly, fast
sorgfältig	carefully

Adverbs of time

anfangs	at the beginning
damals	at that (distant) time
diesmal	this time
erstens	firstly
früher	in the past
heutzutage	nowadays
kürzlich	recently
nachher	after that
neulich	recently

nie	never
noch (nicht)	(not) yet
noch einmal	one more time
noch nie	never
schließlich	finally
täglich	daily
vorher	previously
mit Verspätung	late
im Moment	at the moment, currently

Adverbs of degree

etwa	about
extra *inv*	specially
extrem	extremely
fast	almost, nearly
insgesamt	altogether
kaum	hardly, scarcely
meistens	mostly
mindestens	at least
nur	only
selten	rarely, seldom
total	totally, completely
ungefähr/zirka	about
völlig	entirely
wahrscheinlich	probably
wenig	little, not much
wenigstens	at least

Other adverbs

außerdem	besides
doch	yet, however
bloß	merely
eigentlich	actually
einschließlich	including
im Gegenteil	on the other hand
jedoch	however
so	thus
sonst	otherwise
umsonst	in vain, free of charge
vor allem	above all, especially
zweifellos	doubtless

Verbs

Modal verbs

dürfen *irreg*	to be allowed to
können *irreg*	to be able to, can
mögen *irreg*	to like
müssen *irreg*	to have to, must
sollen *irreg*	to ought to, should
wollen *irreg*	to want to

Essential verbs

hören	to hear
kaufen	to buy
machen	to do, make
sagen	to say, tell
spielen	to play
wohnen	to live
arbeiten †	to work
beginnen *irreg*	to begin
bekommen *irreg*	to get, receive
bringen *irreg*	to bring
essen *irreg*	to eat
fahren* *irreg*	to travel, go
finden *irreg*	to find
gehen* *irreg*	to go
haben *irreg*	to have
kommen* *irreg*	to come
lesen *irreg*	to read
schreiben *irreg*	to write
sehen *irreg*	to see
sein* *irreg*	to be
sprechen *irreg*	to speak, talk
trinken *irreg*	to drink
werden* *irreg*	to become

Very important verbs

brauchen	to need
fragen	to ask
hoffen	to hope
suchen	to look for

bestellen †	to order
besuchen †	to visit
bezahlen †	to pay (for)
enden †	to end, finish
sich interessieren †	to be interested
kosten †	to cost
ankommen* *irreg*	to arrive
aufstehen* *irreg sep*	to get up
bleiben* *irreg*	to stay
geben *irreg*	to give
heißen *irreg*	to be called
laufen* *irreg*	to run
spazieren gehen* *irreg*	to go for a walk
tragen *irreg*	to wear, carry
sich waschen *irreg*	to get washed

Important verbs

dauern	to last
schauen	to look
zeigen	to show
sich amüsieren †	to have a good time
antworten †	to reply, answer
öffnen †	to open
probieren †	to try
tanzen †	to dance
verdienen †	to earn
verkaufen †	to sell
versuchen †	to try
anfangen *irreg*	to begin
denken *irreg*	to think
einladen *irreg sep*	to invite
gewinnen *irreg*	to win
helfen *irreg* (+ Dat)	to help
kennen *irreg*	to know (person)
lassen *irreg*	to let
nehmen *irreg*	to take
schließen *irreg*	to close, shut
schlafen *irreg*	to sleep
schwimmen (*) *irreg* ...	to swim

verbringen *irreg*	to spend (time)
vergessen *irreg*	to forget
verlassen *irreg*	to leave (house)
verlieren *irreg*	to lose
wissen *irreg*	to know (fact)

Useful verbs

anschauen *sep*	to look at
aufhören *sep*	to stop, cease
bauen	to build
blicken	to look (at)
gucken	to watch, look
holen	to fetch
kriegen	to get
lernen	to learn
planen	to plan
weinen	to weep, cry
zählen	to count
begegnen* † (+ Dat).....	to meet, bump into
erklären †	to explain
erzählen †	to tell (story)
küssen †	to kiss
passieren* †	to happen
putzen †	to clean
reisen* †	to travel
reparieren †	to repair
senden †	to send, transmit
warten †	to wait
anhalten *irreg*	to stop
ansehen *irreg*	to look at
bitten *irreg*	to ask (for)
fallen* *irreg*	to fall
geschehen* *irreg*	to happen
halten *irreg*	to hold, keep
rufen *irreg*	to call
singen *irreg*	to sing
sitzen *irreg*	to sit
stehen *irreg*	to stand
treffen *irreg*	to meet
tun *irreg*	to do

Kardinalzahlen   ## Cardinal Numbers

0	null	10	zehn
1	eins	11	elf
2	zwei	12	zwölf
3	drei	13	dreizehn
4	vier	14	vierzehn
5	fünf	15	fünfzehn
6	sechs	16	sechzehn *(no s in the middle)*
7	sieben	17	siebzehn *(no en in the middle)*
8	acht	18	achtzehn
9	neun	19	neunzehn

20   zwanzig
21   einundzwanzig *(no s in the middle)*
22   zweiundzwanzig, etc

30   dreißig *(note the spelling with ß)*
40   vierzig
50   fünfzig
60   sechzig *(no s in the middle)*
70   siebzig *(no en in the middle)*
80   achtzig
90   neunzig
100   hundert
101   hunderteins
102   hundertzwei
141   hunderteinundvierzig
200   zweihundert
999   neunhundertneunundneunzig
1000   tausend
1100   tausendeinhundert/elfhundert/eintausendeinhundert
2002   zweitausendzwei
321 456   dreihunderteinundzwanzigtausendvierhundertsechsundfünfzig
1 000 000   eine Million (spaces every 3 digits, no commas)

Remember that:

1   Years are usually stated in hundreds.
So 1987 = neunzehnhundertsiebenundachtzig

2   Where there is any danger of confusion, *zwo* is used instead of *zwei*.
It is often heard in public announcements, and on the telephone.

3   Longer numbers - such as telephone numbers after dialling codes - are often written and read in pairs. So 01684/57 74 33 is pronounced as:
Null eins sechs acht vier, siebenundfünfzig vierundsiebzig dreiunddreißig.

4   Cardinal numbers can be used as nouns, particularly when discussing school grades.
Example: Ich habe eine Eins in Mathe   *I have a 1 in maths*

Ordinalzahlen

der erste .... first
der zweite.................... second
der dritte...................... third
der vierte...................... fourth
der fünfte .... fifth
der sechste .... sixth
der siebte..................... seventh
der achte...................... eighth
der neunte .... ninth
der zehnte.................... tenth
der elfte....................... eleventh

Ordinal numbers

der zwölfte.................... twelfth
der dreizehnte.............. thirteenth
der vierzehnte.............. fourteenth
der fünfzehnte .... fifteenth
der sechzehnte............. sixteenth
der siebzehnte.............. seventeenth
der achtzehnte .... eighteenth
der neunzehnte .... nineteenth
der zwanzigste............. twentieth
der einundzwanzigste ... twenty-first
der zweiundzwanzigste twenty-second

Die Uhrzeiten

Clock Times

In German, as in English, there are two ways of telling the time, the everyday way and using the 24-hour clock.

12-hour clock (the everyday way)

Es ist ein Uhr	1.00
Es ist fünf Uhr	5.00
Es ist fünf (Minuten) nach fünf	5.05
Es ist Viertel nach fünf	5.15
Es ist halb sechs (*careful!*)	5.30
Es ist Viertel vor sechs	5.45
Es ist fünf (Minuten) vor sechs	5.55
Es ist Mittag/Mitternacht	12.00
Es ist Viertel nach zwölf	12.15

24-hour clock

Es ist ein Uhr	01.00
Es ist fünf Uhr	05.00
Es ist siebzehn Uhr	17.00
Es ist siebzehn Uhr fünf	17.05
Es ist siebzehn Uhr fünfzehn	17.15
Es ist siebzehn Uhr dreißig	17.30
Es ist siebzehn Uhr fünfundvierzig	17.45
Es ist siebzehn Uhr fünfundfünfzig	17.55
Es ist zwölf Uhr	12.00
Es ist null Uhr eins	00.01

Tage und Monate

Montag	Monday
Dienstag	Tuesday
Mittwoch	Wednesday
Donnerstag	Thursday
Freitag	Friday
Samstag	Saturday
Sonnabend	Saturday (North Germany)
Sonntag	Sunday

All days and months are masculine.

am Montag   on Monday
im Februar   in February

Days and months

Januar	January
Februar	February
März	March
April	April
Mai	May
Juni	June
Juli	July
August	August
September	September
Oktober	October
November	November
Dezember	December

When there is any danger of confusion, *Juno* is used for *Juni* and *Julei* for *Juli*.

Daten   ## Dates

Heute haben wir den ersten September .... Today is September 1st
Heute haben wir den zweiten Januar .... Today is January 2nd
Heute haben wir den siebten März .... Today is March 7th
Heute haben wir den fünfundzwanzigsten Mai .... Today is May 25th
Heute haben wir den dreißigsten April .... Today is April 30th
Ich habe am vierten Februar Geburtstag .... My birthday is February 4th
Ich bin neunzehnhundertachtundachtzig geboren .... I was born in 1988

Remember that *'in'* is **not** used with years in German.

Wann?   ## When?

gestern .... yesterday
heute .... today
morgen .... tomorrow

am Vormittag .... in the morning
am Nachmittag .... in the afternoon
am Abend .... in the evening
gestern Abend .... last night
morgen früh .... tomorrow morning

morgens .... in the mornings
mittags .... at midday
nachmittags .... in the afternoons
abends .... in the evenings
nachts .... at night
montags, usw .... on Mondays, etc

jeden Tag .... every day
jeden Morgen .... every morning
jeden Abend .... every evening
jede Woche .... every week
jedes Jahr .... every year

letztes Jahr .... last year
letzte Woche .... last week
nächste Woche .... next week
nächstes Jahr .... next year

im letzten Jahrhundert .. last century
vor einem Jahr .... a year ago
vorgestern .... the day before yesterday
übermorgen .... the day after tomorrow
in zwei Jahren .... in two years' time

Es dauert ...   ## It lasts ...

eine Viertelstunde .... quarter of an hour
eine halbe Stunde .... half an hour
eine Stunde .... an hour
anderthalb Stunden ...... 1½ hours
zwei Stunden .... 2 hours
einen Tag .... a day
zwei Tage .... 2 days
eine Woche .... a week
zwei Wochen .... 2 weeks
einen Monat .... a month
ein Jahr .... a year

Die Jahreszeiten   Seasons

der Frühling .... spring
der Sommer .... summer
der Herbst .... autumn
der Winter .... winter

Mitteleuropa